A Star over Bethlehem

A Star
over Bethlehem

*From Advent
to the
Epiphany*

New City

London   **New York**   **Manila**

First published in 2001
In Great Britain
by
New City
57 Twyford Avenue
London W3 9PZ

Illustrations by Joan Day
Cover design by Nick Cianfarani

A catalogue record for this book
is available from the British Library

ISBN 0 904287 77 7

Scripture quotations are from The New English Bible

Typeset by New City, London
Printed in Canada

Contents

Part 4: All Around the Manger

Part 5: Christmas Stories

Part 6: St Stephen and the Holy Innocents

Part 7: The Epiphany

Part 8: Reflections on the Mystery

Introduction

*T*wo thousand years ago, we are told, a star appeared in the East. Certain wise men understood this to mean that a baby had been born who was to be king over all the world. What was that star? Was it a comet? We don't know, but stars then and today, have always been considered lights to steer by, and the story goes that these wise men were guided to Bethlehem, to one who was to be called the Light of the World.

The images are evocative. The wealth of myths and legends, songs and stories that have grown up around the biblical narrative are witness to that and can be taken on several different levels. In fact, the story leading up to the birth of the child and his manifestation to the world, from advent to the epiphany, are a kind of super-history. Whatever may be the precise and objective historical details of what happened all those long centuries ago, and however much scholars, believers or agnostics may vary in their opinions, this story still speaks powerfully and truthfully to us today. The tale of the past unlocks the meaning of now.

The aim of this collection is, in one sense, to present a journey through the whole sweep of the events surrounding the first Christmas stripped of their tinsel and glitter, without trees and reindeer and Santa Claus, and without the stresses and strains of consumerism, to present them in all their beauty, simplicity and depth. It is to go to the heart of the story by meditating on the images that surround and build it up. This may sound like a paradox, but we know that simplicity is deceptive; it is not easy.

It is hoped that the insights gathered here and expressed in the words of saints and poets and great thinkers may help us in our own meditations and explorations and, not least, be a source of practical inspiration to all those who seek to present any part of the Christmas story – giving pastors, teachers, youth workers and dramatists tools to tell the exquisite tale of God's love for his people. But in the truest sense, also and especially, it is hoped that these insights will give pure enjoyment for, after all, we are told that joy is of the kingdom.

Ann Finch

Part One

Preparing the Way

The Word to be Made Flesh

*T*here appeared a man named John, sent from God;
he came as a witness to testify to the light, that all
might become believers through him.
He was not himself the light;
he came to bear witness to the light.
The real light which enlightens every man
was even then coming into the world.
He was in the world; but the world,
though it owed its being to him,
did not recognise him.
He entered his own realm,
and his own would not receive him.
But to all who did receive him,
to those who have yielded him their allegiance,
he gave the right to become children of God,
not born of any human stock,
or by the fleshly desire of a human father,
but the offspring of God himself.
So the Word became flesh;
he came to dwell among us,
and we saw his glory,
such glory as befits the Father's only Son,
full of grace and truth.

John 1: 6-14

Then Will Be the End

*W*e are sometimes inclined to think that the same things are monotonously repeated over and over again in the history of creation. That is because the season is too long by comparison with the brevity of our individual lives, and the transformation too vast and too inward by comparison with our superficial and restricted outlook, for us to see the progress of what is tirelessly taking place to and through all matter and all spirit. Let us believe in Revelation, once again our faithful support in our most human forebodings. Under the commonplace envelope of things and of all our purified and salvaged efforts, a new earth is being slowly engendered.

One day, the Gospel tells us, the tension gradually accumulating between humanity and God will touch the limits prescribed by the possibilities of the world. And then will come the end. Then the presence of Christ, which has been silently accruing in things, will suddenly be revealed – like a flash of light from pole to pole. Breaking through all the barriers within which the veil of matter and the water-tightness of souls have seemingly kept it confined, it will invade the face of the earth. And under the finally-liberated action of the true affinities of being, the spiritual atoms of the world will be borne along by a force generated by the powers of cohesion proper to the universe itself, and will occupy, whether within Christ or without Christ (but always under the influence of Christ), the place of happiness or pain designated for them by the living structure of the Pleroma. 'As the lightning comes from the east and shines as far as the west... as the flood came and swept them all away... so will be the coming of the Son of Man' (Matt. 24:27,39). Like lightning, like a conflagration, like a flood, the attraction exerted by the Son of Man will lay hold of all the whirling elements in the universe so as to reunite them or subject them to his body. 'Wherever the body is, there will the eagles be gathered together.'

Such will be the consummation of the divine *milieu*.

As the Gospel warns us, it would be vain to speculate as to the hour and the modalities of this formidable event. But we have to *expect* it.

Expectation – anxious, collective and operative expectation of an end of the world, that is to say of an issue for the world – that is perhaps the supreme Christian function and the most distinctive characteristic of our religion.

Teilhard de Chardin
(1881 – 1955)

The Trinity
Has Thrown Open Its Gates

*I*t is mysterious and momentous
that the second Person of the Most Holy Trinity
became incarnate,
through which, for all eternity, our human nature
is inseparably placed
in the heart of God.
It is mysterious and goes beyond our reasoning.
God in his second Person,
will never more be parted from human nature in Jesus!

If the Most Holy Trinity has thrown open its gates so
         that the Word
could become human for us,
we are crazy if we do not believe
in the love of God for everyone.

Chiara Lubich

To Bring Salvation

*T*he Lord of the world did not consider it right
to allow human beings, for love of whom everything had
    been made,
to be besieged by sin and to be sold like slaves to death.
For this reason he assumed human form,
hid his invisible nature under visible guise,
and kept the visible nature free from the stain of sin.
Undoubtedly, it would have been easy for him
to save the human race without assuming the garment of
    the flesh.
He could have overthrown the power of death by a simple
    act of will.
He could have made the father of that power, sin,
disappear by exiling it from earth in such a way
that no trace of it would remain on the earth.
Instead of that, he chose to demonstrate the holiness of his
    providential care.
To restore salvation to human beings
he did not employ as his servants the angels and archangels,
nor cause a piercing voice to resound from heaven.
He preferred to build for himself a chamber in the womb of
    the Virgin
and from there to come among us.
For this reason we think of him as man and adore him as God.
Begotten of the Father before the beginning of time,
he took of the Virgin a visible body.
He is the Being who is both new and pre-existent.

Theodoret, Bishop of Cyrrhus
(393 – 460)

A Paradox

*C*hristmas is drawing near. For a man who sees with only one eye what is approaching is cold, darkness and hunger. For the man who sees things in God, with both the human and the divine eye, the Redemption is approaching, which is joy, life and deification.

Christmas, an image of the paradox that the Redemption constitutes for men. It reveals the ways in which the heavenly Father acts, who makes of a stable the abode of the Eternal, the meeting-place of purity and beauty. He can make the God-Man come to birth in the bare and tattered dwelling of an old man, a person who is the temple of the Holy Spirit, if he wishes, and so a meeting-place for angels singing to the universe.

Igino Giordani
(1894 – 1980)

The God Who Comes

*W*hat are these people, His People, looking for in Him?
What characteristics do they expect when they see Him for
    the first time?
Power, glory, blinding light, triumph.
What happens?
Weakness, smallness, obscurity, anonymity.
Who cared about God's coming, veiled in the flesh of a
defenceless child?
No one!
Mary, the poor mother of Jesus, clasps in her arms the '
    Unknown
One' of the people, the true 'Hidden God' of Isaiah.
Those who were waiting were blind.
Nobody moved from Jerusalem, the holy city, the footstool
of the throne of God!
No, worse! Someone did move, but only in order to murder
    this nuisance who had not come in the way He was
    expected.
The most religious people on earth, the Chosen People, were
    living only on that waiting, and it had become spas
    modic, it could be felt in the air.
What were they searching the horizon for, at the advent of
    the Messiah, at the dawn of all the prophecies?
The son of David, the conqueror, the God of Hosts, He who
    was to restore the Kingdom, He who would finally
    oppress the hated Romans! Triumph, victory, safety
    … always the same!
What happened?
A poor workman, hidden in an unknown village – and the
most despised one at that.

No good. After so many years, no one realised what had
    happened.
Their eyes were searching for something quite different than
the sweat of a labourer or the anonymity of a poor man!
And how does the story end?
The clash between Him who says He is the Son of God, the
    Messiah, and those who cannot accept such goings
    on reaches a climax; it closes with the crucifixion of
    an innocent man.
Bethlehem, Nazareth, Calvary are demonstrations of God's
    silence and God's poverty, real roads that He trav
    elled in order tocome to us and to make Himself
    known.
And they are darkness.
Oh, not darkness for Him, or in themselves, for nothing is
    more luminous than the annihilation of Jesus at
    Bethlehem, the reality of the incarnation at
    Nazareth, the infinite love streaming from Calvary.
That is light, and what light!
But for us, who want noise, God is silence; the light is darkness.
Darkness for us who want power, while God is meekness.
Darkness for us who want pleasure, always pleasure, while
God is service and gratitude and love, often painful love.

Carlo Carretto
(1910 – 1988)

A Jewish Girl

We, with our modern democratic and arithmetical presuppositions would so have liked and expected all men to start equal in their search for God. One has the picture of great centripetal roads coming from all directions, with well-disposed people, all meaning the same thing, and getting closer and closer together. How shockingly opposite to that is the Christian story! One people picked out of the whole earth; that people purged and proved again and again. Some are lost in the desert before they reach Palestine; some stay in Babylon; some becoming indifferent. The whole thing narrows and narrows, until at last it comes down to a little point, small as the point of a spear – a Jewish girl at her prayers. That is what the whole of human nature has narrowed down to before the Incarnation takes place. Very unlike what we expected, but, of course, not in the least unlike what seems, in general, as shown by Nature, to be God's way of working.... The people who are selected are, in a sense, unfairly selected for a supreme honour; but it is also a supreme burden. The People of Israel come to realise that it is their woes which are saving the world.

C.S. Lewis
(1898 – 1963)

Building a Palace

I magine yourself as a living house. God comes in to rebuild that house. At first, perhaps, you can understand what He is doing. He is getting the drains right and stopping the leaks in the roof and so on: you knew that those jobs needed doing and so you are not surprised. But presently He starts knocking the house about in a way that hurts abominably and does not seem to make sense. What on earth is He up to? The explanation is that He is building quite a different house from the one you thought of – throwing out a new wing here, putting on an extra floor there, running up towers, making courtyards. You thought you were going to be made into a decent little cottage: but He is building a palace. He intends to come and live in it Himself.

C.S. Lewis
(1898 – 1963)

The Way Things Work Now

*T*he Son of God became a man to enable men to become sons of God. We do not know – anyway, I do not know – how things would have worked if the human race had never rebelled against God and joined the enemy. Perhaps every man would have been 'in Christ', would have shared the life of the Son of God, from the moment he was born. Perhaps the *Bios* or natural life would have been drawn up into the *Zoe*, the uncreated life, at once and as a matter of course. But that is guesswork. You and I are concerned with the way things work now.

And the present state of things is this. The two kinds of life are now not only different (they would always have been that) but actually opposed. The natural life in each of us is something self-centred, something that wants to be petted and admired, to take advantage of other lives, to exploit the whole universe. And especially it wants to be left to itself: to keep well away from anything better or stronger or higher than it, anything that might make it feel small. It is afraid of the light and air of the spiritual world, just as people who have been brought up to be dirty are afraid of a bath. And in a sense it is quite right. It knows that if the spiritual life gets hold of it, all its self-centredness and self-will are going to be killed, and it is ready to fight tooth and nail to avoid that.

C.S. Lewis
(1898 – 1963)

23

The Annunciation

*I*n the sixth month the angel Gabriel was sent from God to a town in Galilee called Nazareth, with a message for a girl betrothed to a man named Joseph, a descendant of David; the girl's name was Mary. The angel went in and said to her, 'Greetings, most favoured one! The Lord is with you.' But she was deeply troubled by what he said and wondered what this greeting might mean. Then the angel said to her, 'Do not be afraid Mary, for God has been gracious to you; you shall conceive and bear a son, and you shall give him the name Jesus. He will be great; he will bear the title "Son of the Most High"; the Lord God will give him the throne of his ancestor David, and he will be king over Israel for ever; his reign shall never end.' 'How can this be,' said Mary, 'when I have no husband?' The angel answered, 'The Holy Spirit will come upon you; and the power of the Most High will overshadow you; and for that reason the holy child to be born will be called "Son of God".' 'Here am I,' said Mary; 'I am the Lord's servant; as you have spoken, so be it.'

Luke 1: 26-38

Gabriel's Song

*G*abriel was invited to Nazareth to bring to the Virgin the glad annunciation from the Father. The angel found Mary at home and greeted her with these words:

"Rejoice, you that are full of grace; the Lord is with you.
Rejoice, you that are the first and only one to conceive a babe
    free from sin.
Rejoice, you that bring into the world the beginning of life.
Rejoice, O Virgin Mother.
Rejoice, O Mother unmarried yet not without child.
Rejoice, O Mother unwed but not unfruitful.
Rejoice, you that await the birth yet shall not travail.
Rejoice, you that bear the deliverer from your father Adam.
Rejoice, you that without wearying sustain the sustainer of
    creation.
Rejoice, you that without pain are intermediary between
    God and humanity.
Rejoice, you that give birth to a God who is not only God,
    to a man who is not just a man.
Rejoice, you that are full of grace: the Lord is with you."

The Virgin did not give importance to the exhortation to rejoice but reflected on this greeting and said: "What can this salutation be? And who is this who entered our home without an invitation?"

The angel explained: "Fear not, Mary. You have acquired the grace that the first woman lost. She, alone, yielded to the tempter's guile. Now you, alone, are bearing the conqueror of temptation. You will bring forth a son and shall call his name Jesus."

Antipater of Bostra (d. 375)

The Virgin Mary
and the Air We Breathe

I say that we are wound
With mercy round and round
As if with air: the same
Is Mary, more by name.
She, wild web, wondrous robe,
Mantles the guilty globe,
Since God has let dispense
Her prayers his providence:
Nay, more than almoner,
The sweet alms' self is her
And men are meant to share
Her life as life does air.

Gerard Manley Hopkins
(1844 – 1889)

Part Two

My Soul Magnifies the Lord

The Mother of the Lord

*T*he resemblance between the *Magnificat* and traditional Hebrew poetry ... is not mere literary curiosity. There is, of course, a difference. There are no cursings here, no hatred, no self-righteousness. Instead, there is mere statement. He has scattered the proud, cast down the mighty, sent the rich empty away. I spoke ? of the ironic contrast between the fierce psalmists and the choirboy's treble. The contrast is here brought up to a higher level. Once more we have the treble voice, a girl's voice, announcing without sin that the sinful prayers of her ancestors do not remain entirely unheard; and doing this, not indeed with fierce exultation, yet – who can mistake the tone? – in a calm and terrible gladness...

Christians are unhappily divided about the kind of honour in which the Mother of the Lord should be held, but there is one truth about which no doubt seems admissible. If we believe in the Virgin Birth and if we believe in Our Lord's human nature, psychological as well as physical (for it is heretical to think Him a human body which had the Second Person of the Trinity *instead of* a human soul) we must also believe in a human heredity for that human nature. There is only one source for it (though in that source all the true Israel is summed up). If there is an iron element in Jesus may we not without irreverence guess whence, humanly speaking, it came? Did neighbours say, in His boyhood, 'He's His Mother's Son'? This might set in a new and less painful light the severity of some things He said to, or about His Mother. We may suppose that she understood them very well.

C. S. Lewis (1898 – 1963)

The Visitation

Our Lady did not go to Elizabeth to sing the Magnificat but to help her. In the same way, we must not go to our neighbours to reveal to them the spiritual treasure we carry in our hearts, but to share with them their sorrows and burdens, their joys and responsibilities.

If we do this perfectly the time will soon come when we shall be able to open our hearts in order to share our spiritual riches with our neighbours. Then, together with them, we will he able to love the One who has shown us how to treat one another as brothers and sisters.

Chiara Lubich

The Magna Carta

*T*he Magna Carta of Christian social doctrine began with the words of Mary: "He has put down the mighty from their thrones, and exalted the lowly; he has filled the hungry with good things, and sent the rich away empty-handed" (Lk. 1: 52-53).

The greatest and most sweeping revolution of all times is contained in the Gospel.

Perhaps it is part of God's plan that in this age, deeply concerned as it is with social problems, it should be Our Lady to help all of us build, consolidate, raise up, and show the world a new society in which the powerful words of the Magnificat will re-echo.

Chiara Lubich

Mary's Faith

*B*ut Mary kept all these words, pondering them in her heart.' Little is told us in Scripture concerning the Blessed Virgin, but there is one grace of which the Evangelists make her the pattern in a few simple sentences – of Faith.

Zacharias questioned the Angel's message, but Mary said, "Behold the handmaid of the Lord; be it done to me according to thy word."

Accordingly Elizabeth, speaking with an apparent allusion to the contrast thus exhibited between her and the highly-favoured Virgin Mary, said, on receiving her salutation, "Blessed art thou among women, and blessed is the fruit of thy womb. Blessed art thou that believed, because those things shall be accomplished that were spoken to thee by the Lord."

But Mary's faith did not end in a mere acquiescence in Divine providences and revelations: as the text informs us, she pondered them.

When the shepherds came, and told of the vision of Angels which they had seen at the time of the Nativity, and how one of them announced that the Infant in her arms was the "Saviour, who is Christ the Lord," while others did but wonder, 'Mary kept all these words pondering them in her heart.'

John Henry Newman
(1801 – 1890)

In Praise of Mary

O Mary, artist of life, hail!
By recreating wholeness, you have convulsed death itself.
You have destroyed the serpent which, blown up with pride,
raised its outstretched neck to Eve.
You have trampled on it by giving birth out of heaven
to God's Son,
breathed into you by the Spirit of God.
O loveliest and most loving Mother, hail!
You have given forth into this world your Son,
sent from heaven and breathed into you by the Spirit of God.
Praised be the Father, the Son, and Holy Spirit.
Breathed into you by the Holy Spirit.

Hildegard of Bingen
(1098 – 1179)

Joseph

*W*ho has not carolled Mary,
 And who her praise would dim?
But what of humble Joseph:
 Is there no song for him?

If Joseph had not driven
 Straight nails through honest wood;
If Joseph had not cherished
 His Mary as he should;

If Joseph had not proved him
 A sire both kind and wise:
Would he have drawn with favour
 The Child's all-probing eyes?

Would Christ have prayed "Our Father",
 Or cried that Name in death,
Unless he first had honoured
 Joseph of Nazareth?

Gilbert Thomas

In the Carpenter's Shop

I wish I had been His apprentice
To see Him each morning at seven,
As He tossed His grey tunic about Him,
The Master of earth and of heaven;

When He lifted the lid of His work-chest
And opened his carpenter's kit,
And looked at His chisels and augers,
And took the bright tools out of it;

When He gazed at the rising sun tinting
The dew on the opening flowers,
And He smiled at the thought of His Father
Whose love floods this fair world of ours;

When He fastened the apron about Him,
And put on his workingman's cap,
And grasped the smooth shaft of His hammer
To give the bent woodwork a tap,

Saying, "Lad, let us finish this ox yoke,
The farmer must finish his crop."
Oh, I wish I had been His apprentice
And worked in the Nazareth shop.

Anonymous

From the Womb of a Woman

A God who was not only God, and a man who was not simply man, was born of woman.

By being born he formed the gate of salvation from what had at one time been the way in for sin. Where in fact the serpent by exploiting human disobedience had infused his poison, there the Word entered through obedience and built a living temple. From the womb of a woman had come forth the original son of sin, Cain; and from the womb of a woman, without seed, there came into the light the Christ, the redeemer of the human race.

Let us not be ashamed that he was born of a woman. That birth was for us the beginning of salvation.

If Christ had not been born of woman, he would not have died either, and would not 'by death have destroyed him who had the power of death, that is, the devil.' (Heb. 2: 14)

Proclus of Constantinople
(d. 446)

Part Three

Nativity

The Incomprehensibility of God

*T*he Inaccessible
comes down to us by love:
the Son,
the invisible image of God,
makes himself visible
through the Incarnation.

To see God is to meet Christ
in one's neighbour.

John Chrysostom
(d. 407)

Christmas Daybreak

B efore the paling of the stars,
    Before the winter morn,
Before the earliest cockcrow,
    Jesus Christ was born:
Born in a stable,
    Cradled in a manger,
In the world His hands had made,
    Born a stranger.

Priest and king lay fast asleep
    In Jerusalem,
Young and old lay fast asleep
    In crowded Bethlehem:
Saint and angel, ox and ass,
    Kept a watch together,
Before the Christmas daybreak
    In the winter weather.

Jesus on His Mother's breast,
    In the stable cold,
Spotless Lamb of God was He,
    Shepherd of the fold.
Let us kneel with Mary Maid,
    With Joseph bent and hoary,
With saint and angel, ox and ass,
    To hail the King of Glory.

Christina Georgina Rossetti
(1830 – 1894)

The Coming of the Lord

*J*ust as, on the factual side, a long preparation culminates in God's becoming incarnate as Man, so, on the documentary side, the truth first appears in *mythical* form and then by a long process of condensing or focusing finally becomes incarnate as History. This involves the belief that Myth is … a real though unfocused gleam of divine truth falling on human imagination. The Hebrews, like other peoples, had mythology: but as they were the chosen people so their mythology was the chosen mythology – the mythology chosen by God to be the vehicle of the earliest sacred truths, the first step in that process which ends in the New Testament where truth has become completely historical.

C.S. Lewis
(1898 – 1963)

Incarnation Transcends Myth

*N*ow as myth transcends thought, Incarnation transcends myth. The heart of Christianity is a myth which is also a fact. The old myth of the Dying God, *without ceasing to be myth*, comes down from the heaven of legend and imagination to the earth of history. It *happens* – at a particular date, in a particular place, followed by definable historical consequences. We pass from a Balder or an Osiris, dying nobody knows when or where, to a historical Person crucified (it is all in order) *under Pontius Pilate*...

Those who do not know that this great myth became Fact when the Virgin conceived are, indeed, to be pitied. But Christians also need to be reminded ... that what became Fact was a Myth, that it carries with it into the world of fact all the properties of a myth. God is more than a god, not less; Christ is more than Balder, not less. We must not be ashamed of the mythical radiance resting on our theology. We must not be nervous about 'parallels' and 'Pagan Christs': they *ought* to be there – it would be a stumbling block if they weren't.

C.S. Lewis
(1898 – 1963)

When Time Altered Course

'In the night of the year naught, at the moment when Time altered course, God overturned the established order, and chose, once and for all, the 'little ones'.

According to human standards established over the centuries by Power and Wealth, Joseph is not a celebrity, but a nobody. He might have been a descendant of King David – but now he is a carpenter in Nazareth. He travels on foot: from Nazareth to Bethlehem, from Bethlehem to Egypt, from Egypt to Nazareth, always on foot. Nowadays, Joseph travels by Tube: standing, silent, his face ashen with tiredness, but easy to recognise by his look and his smile.

Mary travels second class and she does not worry that the seats are hard. There's a tiny baby crying, and some soldiers on leave are playing the harmonica in the corridor. The kingdom of the little people, the kingdom of Mary and Joseph is like this. And God knows what he is doing when he invites the shepherds before anyone else. They prepare themselves in the silence of the Bethlehem night, to be the first to take part in the world's greatest story – in fact its only one. Everyone, apart from a few specialists, can live perfectly well without thinking about Alexander or Napoleon. But there are about a billion people in the world who every day live in spirit some event from that story which began in this silent Judean night. And this has been going on for twenty centuries.

When the King of Kings was born, he chose his parents from among the little people of this world. And the little people of the district were the first he invited to his cradle – those who slept under the stars of heaven and could hear the angel's voice. It was only then that he received the great ones of the world. They were also his children, but their lives were threatened by glory and honour. He called them, but they were so far off that the journey took them a long time. Those mighty kings announced their arrival with expensive presents. But first they kneeled down – humility was their real gift.

They kneeled down after the shepherds. That is how Christmas was and that is how it will be until the end of the world.

Gilbert Cesbron

As Joseph Was a-Walkin'

As Joseph was a-walkin',
He heard an angel sing,
'This night shall be the birth-night
Of Christ our Heavenly King.

'His birth-bed shall be neither
In house nor in hall,
Nor in the place of paradise
But in the oxen's stall.

'He neither shall be rocked
In silver nor in gold,
But in the wooden manger
That lieth in the mould.

'He neither shall be washen
With white wine nor with red,
But with the fair spring water
That on you shall be shed.

'He neither shall be clothed
In purple nor in pall,
But in the fair, white linen
That usen babies all.'

As Joseph was a-walkin',
Thus did the angel sing,
And Mary's son at midnight
Was born to be our king.

Anonymous

The Hidden Meaning

The gathering of the clans

*T*he first Christmas was a party. Caesar Augustus issued a decree for a general census. Everyone had to go to the town where he belonged, to the home-town of his family. Joseph therefore took Mary to Bethlehem, for that is where his family – the lineage of David – came from. It was to Bethlehem (at the beginning of the barley harvest) that Naomi returned with her daughter-in-law, Ruth, the Moabitess. It was there that Ruth's great-grandson, David, was anointed King in place of Saul. Bethlehem was a little place with a long history.

All the clan of David's lineage collected. Brothers, cousins, second cousins, the whole family got together just like a family wedding or funeral nowadays, only more so. No wonder the local inn was full. Relations who had not met for years exchanged stories and treated the rest to another round of drinks. Without any post to give advance notice of arrival, there must have been plenty of unexpected guests. It was a glorified Bank Holiday.

The Babe of Bethlehem

Joseph and Mary arrived, and Mary obviously needed quiet and some privacy. I like to think the stable was offered out of kindness, not because they were not wanted, but to give them some respite from all the revelry and the comings and goings. It may have been primitive, but at least it was private. How on earth could the inn keeper be expected to know the significance of what was going on in his stable? Considering the dozens of guests, he did his best. In these conditions, Jesus the Christ, the Saviour of the world, the Son of God, was born. Perhaps he was registered in the census, numbered as a member of the family of the clan of David, recorded on a scroll, as years later Pilate put his name down on a list when he was numbered among the transgressors. Probably the inn keeper told all his guests what had happened in the stable. 'Good for you! Good for them! Let's drink the baby's health. Long life and happiness to the latest of the line of David!' How could they be expected to know?

The only people who knew what had really happened were Joseph and Mary. The greatest event in human history happened in secret. Two people only (or four, if you count Elisabeth and John) understood the secret. Much the same applied to the Temptations, the Transfiguration, the agony in the Garden of Gethsemane, the Resurrection and the Ascension. Only the Crucifixion was open to public human view, and that was misunderstood by all except a very few. How silently, how silently the wondrous gift is given.

Unto you is born a Saviour

The irony of it all was that they were looking for a deliverer, someone who would make them free. They would be free from subjection to the very Romans who had ordered the census. If only they had known! But how could they be expected to know? To some shepherds the message came, 'To you is born this day … a Saviour'. They came with joy, hastily, and when they had seen the child they told everyone what they had been told, and at least it made them wonder. But Mary kept all these things and pondered them in her heart.

Christmas is different now? For those who know and understand the secret, yes! Not just the birthday of a child, with celebrations all round and a gathering of the clans. Unto you is born a Saviour. The life given to us at Bethlehem was given for us on Calvary. We keep the Festival with the

Holy Communion where, in a mystery, the life given for us is given back to us. Black and white, western and eastern, rich and poor, all mankind can celebrate this day when the Son of God was born into the human family to make us free.

Author unknown

The Nativity

*P*eace? and to all the world? Sure One,
And He the Prince of Peace, hath none!
He travels to be born, and then
Is born to travel more again.
Poor Galilee! thou canst not be
The place for His Nativity.
His restless mother's call'd away,
And not deliver'd till she pay.

A tax? 'tis so still! we can see
The Church thrive in her misery,
And, like her Head at Bethl'em, rise,
When she, oppressed with troubles, lies.
Rise? – should all fall, we cannot be
In more extremities than He.
Great Type of passions! Come what will,
Thy grief exceeds all copies still.
Thou cam'st from Heav'n to Earth, that we
Might go from Earth to Heav'n with Thee:
And though Thou found'st no welcome here,
Thou didst provide us mansions there.

A stable was Thy Court, and when
Men turned to beasts, beasts would be men:
They were Thy courtiers; others none;
And their poor manger was Thy throne.
No swaddling silks Thy limbs did fold.
Though Thou could'st turn Thy rays to gold.
No rockers waited on Thy birth,
No cradles stirred, nor songs of mirth;

But her chaste lap and sacred breast,
Which lodged Thee first, did give Thee rest.

But stay: what light is that doth stream
And drop here in a gilded beam?
It is Thy star runs page, and brings
Thy tributary Eastern kings.
Lord! grant some light to us, that we
May with them find the way to Thee!
Behold what mists eclipse the day!
How dark it is! Shed down one ray,
To guide us out of this dark night,
And say once more, "Let there be light!"

Henry Vaughan 1656
(1622 – 1695)

My Own Christmas Day

*C*hristmas, feast of the birth of Jesus, is for me the reply of
        God and the Church to a need of the soul:
to hear repeated to me every year, through the commemo
        ration of that fact so sweet, so sublime,
so simple and so deep,
that God loves me.

Yes, if in my existence, I am able to fulfil my deepest aspira
        tions,
it is only because God has looked also upon me, as he has
        upon everyone, and has become man to give me
the laws of life that, like light on the road,
help me walk safely
towards our common destiny.

But Christmas for me is not just a commemoration, howev
        er meaningful. It is a spur
for me to work to restore the presence of Christ
in the midst of the society in which I live.
He is there where two or more are united in his name (cf.
        Matt. 18: 20), like an everyday spiritual Christmas,
in homes in factories, in schools, in public buildings…
This day of Christmas, furthermore, opens my heart to the
        whole of humanity.
Its warmth goes beyond the Christian world
and seems to invade every land,
a sign that that baby came for everyone.
In fact it is his plan: that all may be one (cf. John 17: 21).

And every Christmas then I always ask myself: 'How many
        more Christmases will I see in my life?'

This question, which has no answer, helps me to live every
        year as if it were the last
with a greater awareness of my own Christmas day,
the 'dies natalis',
the day which will signal for me
the beginning of the life that never dies.

Chiara Lubich

Nativity

The moon is born
and a child is born,
lying among white clothes
as the moon among clouds.

They both shine, but
the light from the one
is abroad in the universe
as among broken glass.

R. S. Thomas
(1913 – 2000)

Part Four

All around the Manger

The Shepherds' Carol

We stood on the hills, Lady,
Our day's work done.
Watching the frosted meadows
That winter had won.

The evening was calm, Lady.
The air so still,
Silence more lovely than music
Folded the hill,

There was a star, Lady,
Shone in the night
Larger than Venus it was
And bright, so bright.

Oh, a voice from the sky, Lady,
It seemed to us then
Telling of God being born
In the world of men.

And so we have come, Lady,
Our day's work done,
Our love, our hopes, ourselves
We give to your son.

Anonymous

The Angels
for the Nativity of Our Lord

Run, shepherds, run where Bethlem blest appears,
We bring the best of news, be not dismayed,
A Saviour there is born more old than years,
Amidst heaven's rolling heights this earth who stayed.
In a poor cottage inned, a virgin maid
A weakling did him bear, who all upbears;
There is he, poorly swaddled, in manger laid,
To whom too narrow swaddlings are our spheres:
Run, shepherds, run, and solemnize his birth,
This is that night – no, day, grown great with bliss,
In which the power of Satan broken is;
In heaven be glory, peace upon the earth!
Thus singing, through the air the angels swam,
And cope of stars re-echoËd the same.

William Drummond
(1585 – 1649)

The Shepherd and the King

*T*he Shepherd and the King,
The Angel and the Ass,
They heard Sweet Mary sing
When her joy was come to pass:
They heard Sweet Mary sing
To the Baby on her knee,
Sing again, Sweet Mary,
And we will sing with thee!

Earth, bear a berry!
Heaven, bear a light!
Man, make you merry
On Christmas night.

The oxen in the stall,
The sheep upon the hill,
They are waking all
To hear Sweet Mary still.
The Baby is a Child
And the Child is running free,
Sing again, Sweet Mary
And we will sing with thee!

The people in the land,
So many million strong,
All silently do stand
To hear Sweet Mary's song.
The Child he is a Man,
And the Man hangs on a tree!
Sing again, Sweet Mary,
And we will sing with thee!

The Stars that are so old,
The grass that is so young,
They listen in the cold
To hear Sweet Mary's tongue.
The Man's the Son of God
And in Heaven walketh He,
Sing again, Sweet Mary,
And we will sing with thee!

Anonymous

A Stable Bare

I saw a stable, low and very bare,
A little child in a manger.
The oxen knew Him, had Him in their care,
To men He was a stranger.
The safety of the world was lying there,
And the world's danger.

Mary Elizabeth Coleridge
(1861 – 1907)

The Barn

"*I* am tired of this barn!" said the colt.
"And every day it snows.
Outside there's no grass any more
And icicles grow on my nose.
I am tired of hearing the cows
Breathing and talking together.
I am sick of these clucking hens.
I hate stables and winter weather!"

"Hush, little colt," said the mare
"And a story I will tell
Of a barn like this one of ours
And the wonders that there befell.
It was weather much like this,
And the beasts stood as we stand now
In the warm good dark of the barn –
A horse and an ass and a cow."

"And sheep?" asked the colt. "Yes, sheep,
And a pig and a goat and a hen.
All of the beasts of the barnyard,
The usual servants of men.
And into their midst came a lady
And she was cold as death,
But the animals leaned above her
And made her warm with their breath.

"There was her baby born
And laid to sleep in the hay,
While music flooded the rafters

And the barn was as light as day.
And angels and kings and shepherds
Came to worship the babe from afar,
But we looked at him first of all creatures
By the bright strange light of a star!"

Elizabeth Coatsworth
(1893 – 1986)

The Burning Babe

As I in hoary winter's night
Stood shivering in the snow,
Surprised I was with sudden heat
Which made my heart to glow;

And lifting up a fearful eye
To view what fire was near,
A pretty babe all burning bright
Did in the air appear;

Who, scorchèd with excessive heat,
Such floods of tears did shed,
As though His floods should quench His flames
Which with His tears were fed.

'Alas!' quoth He, 'but newly born
In fiery heats I fry,
Yet none approach to warm their hearts
Or feel my fire but I.'

'My faultless breast the furnace is;
The fuel wounding thorns;
Love is the fire, and sighs the smoke;
The ashes shame and scorns;

The fuel Justice layeth on,
And Mercy blows the coals,
The metal in this furnace wrought
Are men's defilèd souls:

For which, as now on fire I am
To work them to their good,
So will I melt into a bath,
To wash them in my blood.'

With this He vanished out of sight
And swiftly shrunk away,
And straight I callèd unto mind
That it was Christmas day.

Robert Southwell
(1561 – 1595)

The Oxen

Christmas Eve, and twelve of the clock.
        'Now they are all on their knees,'
An elder said as we sat in a flock
        By the embers in hearth-side ease.

We pictured the meek mild creatures where
        They dwelt in their strawy pen,
Nor did it occur to one of us there
        To doubt they were kneeling then.

So fair a fancy few would weave
        In these years! Yet, I feel,
If someone said on Christmas Eve,
Come, see the oxen kneel

'In the lonely barton by yonder coomb
        Our childhood used to know,'
I should go with him in the gloom,
        Hoping it might be so.

Thomas Hardy
(1840 – 1928)

Part Five

Christmas Stories

Christmas Eve

*I*n spite of all the graces Heaven was showering upon me, I was far from deserving them. I had a great desire for virtue, but all that I did was full of imperfections. I was so sensitive that I was a very great trial to others; it was useless to reason with me, for I was powerless to correct this fault. How could I expect to be received at Carmel? It would need a miracle to make me grow up once and for all, and God worked this little miracle on a date I shall never forget: December 25, 1886. The new-born Child turned my darkness into light; having for my sake become small and weak, He made me strong and brave; He armed me with His own weapons; and after that *I ran my course* like a giant (Ps. 28) going from victory to victory. The fountain of my tears was dried up, and very rarely flowed again.

This is how I received the grace of conversion. They still treated me at home like a baby, filling my shoes with presents and putting them by the fireplace on Christmas Eve. My father had always shared in my delight as I drew out each gift, but this year Our Lord wished to cure me of my childishness. As I went up to my room after midnight Mass, I heard my father say: "Thérèse is too big a girl for such nonsense; I hope this will be the last year." The words cut me to the heart, and Celine, knowing my sensitiveness, begged me not to go down at once, as I would be sure to cry; but I was no longer the same, Jesus had changed my heart. I went down to the dining room as though nothing had happened, and gaily pulled out the presents one by one, my father joining in the merriment. Celine thought that she was dreaming, but the fact remained that I had found once more the fortitude I had lost at the age of four and a half.

On that blessed night the third period of my life opened, the most beautiful and full of graces. The work I had attempted for years, was done in an instant by Our Lord, who accepted my good will. Like the Apostles, I could say: *Master, we have laboured all the night, and have taken nothing* (Luke v, 5), but Our Lord did more for me than He did for them, for He cast the net Himself and drew it in full of fish, and changed me into a fisher of souls. Charity took possession of my soul and filled me with the spirit of self-forgetfulness, and from that time I was always happy.

Thérèse of Lisieux
(1873 – 1897)

Saint Foam and The Holy Child

O n a black horse
A long time ago in a northern forest
Rode Rothga the heathen child.

Rothga, where are you riding?
Said a great witch.
I am not riding to see you,
Said Rothga.

Then came a bear who stood upright
Upon his hind legs: Where are you riding, Rothga,
Not that I mind? Well, not to see you.
And she rode more quickly. Because, she said,
There is not much time.

On, on they went,
The heathen child and her black horse,
Until the forest broke –
And they came to a sea-shore where the great waves
Threw their froth and foam beneath the lights
Of a northern sky.

Rothga left her black horse and ran
Down to the sea's edge. I am in time,
She said, and laughed to see
Riding the greatest of the sea-waves
A Child of Light who cried:
I am new-born tonight, in the city of Bethlehem.
Rothga, be sure who I am.

I am sure, said Rothga. You must bless me.

I bless you Rothga, said the Child. I am come to save
All people from the malign witch,
From the indifferent bear
And from the dark forest.
Rothga, take this foam-curd for a token,
It shall never grow dull or grow less.

Rothga went home and said:
Father, mother, we have been blessed by a sea-child
Who gave me this for a token.

Thus it was there came to be built
As it stands today, the Great Church
Of St Foam and the Holy Child
On a northern shore.

Stevie Smith

The Present

I was eight years old, but I was old enough to realise that Christmas presents were not brought by Father Christmas. In our house there was a lot to be done and my parents were completely absorbed in their duties and did not have time to think of little things. Even Christmas presents were collected at the last possible moment.

That Christmas Eve I was alone in the house awaiting my father and mother. I remember I was in front of the stove, where I had just gone to prepare some food, when my parents came home. As soon as they saw me they started to sympathise with me. My father stroked my hair. I heard my mother say something about 'the poor child'.

At first I did not understand, then I did not want to understand. A little confused, they said: "You know how busy we have been. Now we have something unpleasant to tell you. We have not had time to go to the shops to buy you a present. We have only just finished working, and its eight o'clock. But when they open again we will buy whatever you want."

I felt a terrible suffering which struck right to my heart. I did not want to believe them. I burst into tears and ran to my bedroom. I cried because I did not have a Christmas present and I could see what would happen the following day when I met my little friends who lived near me. They would ask: "What did Father Christmas bring you?" Then they would show me all the presents they had received, and I would have to reply, "Nothing."

The following year at the same time, Christmas Eve, again I was awaiting alone. Again they were late and I said to myself, "You will see, they will forget again." It seemed that a cynicism, rare at my age, had taken hold of me.

What should I do? I could not bear the thought of suffering

as I did last year. Suddenly I remembered something I had seen a short time before.

A woman had come to do the washing and she had brought her baby girl, about three years old. The child had no shoes although it was winter. She wore tiny wooden clogs and a little apron over a discoloured dress. She sat on the stairs at my house. I was doing some work, but every now and then I looked at her. She was silent, gazing into space, very calm. Suddenly she did a very strange thing. She took off one of her clogs, wrapped it in a filthy handkerchief, then held it in her arms as if it were a doll, rocked it, humming gently.

Following on this memory another thought came to me. "Perhaps there is a way to be happy even when you are disappointed. Perhaps the only way to be happy is to make others happy."

I rushed to my room, opened a box in which I kept my dolls. Some had lost their arms, or legs, or head, but some were still very pretty. There was one, my favourite, which fascinated me because it was in a little basket and it had a set of clothes which I could change – bonnets, jackets, etc. I looked at it, collected its bits and pieces, put it into a little cot and made a parcel of it.

I rushed around to find the lady before my parents came home. The lady recognised me and said: "What do you want miss?" "It's for your little girl." I turned and ran off. She stood at the door and called after me, "Thanks!"

I arrived home breathless. My parents had still not arrived. Even before I saw them I realised that I had guessed right. They had forgotten my present again. But I only had one thought in my head: that little child.

My parents sympathised with me, but I did not cry. I had a lump in my throat, but I continued to think of that girl, who would be happy. It was the first time in my life that I experienced joy while not receiving anything.

Told by Dori Zamboni

Christmas under Martial Law

*T*he thirteenth of December 1981 was a dark day in the history of Poland, General Jaruzelski imposed martial law on the country, thereby beginning the 'long Polish winter' of 1981-2.

I was in Wroclaw, in south-west Poland at the time. Officially I was there to do some research on the history of Silesia. December 13th was a Sunday and we had just come to the end of a congress for young committed Christians from all over Poland when the news broke. The imposition of martial law meant a heavy military and police presence on the streets, severe restrictions on entering and leaving the country, mass arrests, telephone lines cut, letters censored and countless other restrictions on personal freedom.

Suddenly all our hopes for a new freedom and democracy in Poland, which had been growing since Solidarity had been set up in August 1980, came crashing down. Many of the young people at the congress were members of Solidarity and all of us felt shocked and enraged at the government's action.

It felt as if everything was crumbling, but our faith convinced us that, out of the ruins, God would draw something new and positive. Despite the desperation we felt, we simply had to believe that God had a plan for us and for our country. Things got rapidly worse. In the first few days of martial law thousands of people were arrested, interned in prison camps and interrogated. Food rationing was introduced and fuel for heating was very difficult to get hold of.

For various reasons, that Christmas I found myself completely on my own. It was bitterly cold, and as I tried to come to terms with the situation I thought of Edith Stein, whose house was just near where I was staying. I set off for an ancient little chapel in the middle of the forest. There was a full moon, and the light seemed to intensify the cold. The frost crackled underfoot as the temperature dropped to minus 10 centigrade. Radio broadcasts from the West spoke of 50,000 arrests. Already many of my friends and colleagues from the university had been taken away by the police in the middle of the night and I had no idea where they were. I was filled with fear and uncertainty.

I arrived at the chapel a good half-hour before the start of midnight mass. So many people had come that three or four hundred had to stay outside, following the proceedings with the aid of a loudspeaker. The mass began, and as it went on I had to shuffle about just to keep the circulation going, whereas the people remained completely still. I admired their fortitude. And there in the middle of a forest in a country in the grip of an authoritarian regime, I felt the full power of the miracle of Christmas, the coming of Jesus the light of the world, as I had never felt it before. I was filled with a joy that I had never experienced before and I saw the same joy too reflected on the faces of everyone around me. The loneliness I had felt just a short time ago disappeared and I knelt in that tiny chapel and thanked God for everything he had given me.

Miguel Novak

They Have Evicted Jesus

*I*t's nearly Christmas and the city streets are covered in lights.
A never-ending row of shops, a sophisticated but exorbit
ant richness. To the left of our car a row of shop win
dows catches our attention. Through the window it
is snowing gently: an optical illusion. Boys and girls
on sledges pulled by reindeer and Disney animals.
Still more sledges and Father Christmas and little
deer, piglets, hares, frogs, puppets and red dwarfs.
Everything is moving gracefully. Ah! There are the angels...
But no! They are fairies, recently invented to adorn
the snow-white scene.
A child with his parents stands on tiptoe and watches, fas
cinated.
But in my heart is disbelief and then, almost, rebellion: this
rich world has trapped Christmas and all that goes
with it, and has evicted Jesus!
It loves the poetry, the atmosphere, the friendship that
Christmas brings, the gifts it suggests, the lights, the
stars, the songs. It looks to Christmas for the best
profits of the year. But to Jesus it gives no thought.
'He came to his own home and his own people received him
not...'
'There was no room for him in the inn...',
no, and not even at Christmas.

Last night I didn't sleep. This thought kept me awake. If I
were to be born again, I would do many things. I
would found a Work at the service of the
Christmases of all people on earth; I would print the
most beautiful cards in the world; I would produce

statues, large and small, of the most tasteful art; I would record poems and songs, past and present; I would illustrate books for children and adults on this 'mystery of love'; I would write scripts for plays and films.

I don't know what I would do...

Today I thank the Church for having saved the images.

Years ago, when I was in a country dominated by atheism, a priest was carving sculptures of angels to remind people of heaven. Today I understand him better. The practical atheism, which is now invading the whole world, demands it. Certainly, keeping Christmas while banning the New-born causes sadness.

Let us, at least in our own homes, shout out Who is born, celebrating his coming as never before.

Chiara Lubich

No Room at the Inn

W hat though there be no room for him in the inn? I hope there is in our houses for him. It is Christmas time, and let us keep open house for him; let his rags be our Christmas raiment, his manger our Christmas cheer, his stable our Christmas great chamber, hall, dining room. We must clothe with him, and feed with him, and lodge with him at this feast. He is now ready, by and by, to give us himself to eat; you may see him wrapped ready in the swaddling clothes of his blessed sacrament; you may behold him laid upon the altar as in his manger. Do but make room for him and we will bring him forth, and you shall look upon him and handle him, and feed upon him; bring me only the rags of a rent and torn and broken and contrite heart, the white linen cloths of pure intentions and honest affections to swathe him in, wrap him up fast, and lay him close to our souls and bosoms. It is a day of mysteries: it is a mysterious business we are about; Christ wrapped up, Christ in the sacrament, Christ in a mystery; let us be content to let it go so, believe, admire and adore it.

Mark Frank
(1613 – 1664)

Christmas Passion

$\mathcal{H}$ave you ever done what your better judgement said you should not do? Most of us have at one time or another. Well, let me play the 'Grinch' tonight and confess that what we did at the opening of our mass this evening and will do at all the Christmas masses – namely, have sweet little shepherds install the baby doll Jesus into the manger – was against my better judgement. It was against my better judgement because, touching as it is, it gives the wrong message, which is to focus on the sentimentality of the little baby. And who of us did not nudge our neighbour and whisper, "Isn't that darling? Isn't that cute?" even though, as a matter of record, the baby Jesus has no role in the gospel narrative.

So you say, "Well, what is the right message?" The right message, I repeat, is not a soft, darling baby. The right message is a fierce and a passionate God. The Christmas message and the Christmas celebration is God's great zeal for us, the commitment not to leave us abandoned. It comes down to that: not to leave us in the darkness of political, social, or personal tyrannies. The message of Christmas is summed up in that communication the angel made to Mary at the Annunciation when he made a play on words. He said, "You shall call his name Jesus and he shall be nicknamed Emmanuel, which translates 'God with us'." What you have, then, in Christmas is a terrible desire on God's part to 'be with us', to be a part of the human condition: our losses, our recessions, our disappointed and fractured relationships; the deaths we've had in the past year; the difficulties, the addictions, the alcohol, the drugs, sex; things that turn us upside down a great deal. In all of our entire human condition, the Christmas message is that God doesn't want to let us alone but wants to reach out and be with us. God, the most passionate of Lovers, wants to be Emmanuel.

Let me restate this by sharing a true story. The story mentions a baby because it's told by a woman, the baby's mother, but the point of the story lies far beyond the baby. It tells of God's passion for us. Here is this mother's story:

It was Sunday, Christmas. Our family had spent a holiday in San Francisco with my husband's parents, but in order for us to be back at work on Monday, we found ourselves driving the 400 miles back home to Los Angeles on Christmas Day.

We stopped for lunch in King City. The restaurant was nearly empty. We were the only family and ours were the only children.

I heard Erik, my one year old squeal with glee. 'Hi-there', the two words he always thought were one. 'Hi-there', and he pounded his fat baby hands – whack, whack, whack – on the metal high chair. His face was alive with excitement, his eyes were wide, gums bared in a toothless grin. He wriggled and giggled, and then I saw the source of his merriment. And my eyes could not take it in all at once.

A tattered rag of a coat, obviously bought by someone else eons ago, dirty, greasy, and worn; baggy pants; spindly body; toes that poked out of would-be shoes; a shirt that had ring-around-the-collar all over; and a face like none other – gums as bare as Erik's.

"Hi there, baby. Hi there, big boy, I see ya, Buster."

My husband and I exchanged a look that was a cross between 'What do we do?' and 'Poor devil'.

Our meal came and the banging and the noise continued. Now the old bum was shouting across the room, "Do you know patty cake? Attaboy. Do you know peek-a-boo? Hey, look! He knows peek-a boo!"

Erik continued to laugh and answer, "Hi-there." Every call was echoed. Nobody thought it was cute. The guy was a drunk and a disturbance. I was embarrassed. My husband, Dennis, was humiliated. Even our six year old said, "Why is that old man talking so loud?"

Dennis went to pay the check, imploring me to get Erik and meet him in the parking lot. "Lord, just let me get out of here before he speaks to me or Erik," and I bolted for the door. It soon was obvious that both the Lord and Erik had other plans.

As I drew closer to the man, I turned my back, walking to side-step him and any air that he might be breathing. As I did so, Erik, all the while with his eyes riveted to his best friend, leaned over my arm, reaching with both arms to a baby's pick-me-up position. In a split-second of balancing my baby and turning to counter his weight, I came eye-to-eye with the old man.

Erik was lunging for him, arms spread wide. The bum's eyes both asked and implored, "Would you let me hold your baby?" There was no need for me to answer since Erik propelled himself from my arms to the man. Suddenly a very old man and a very young baby consummated their love relationship.

Erik laid his tiny head upon the man's ragged shoulder. The man's eyes closed and I saw tears hover beneath the lashes. His aged hands, full of grime and pain and hard labour, gently, so gently, cradled my baby's bottom and stroked his back. I stood awestruck.

The old man rocked and cradled Erik in his arms for a moment, and then his eyes opened and set squarely on mine. He said in a firm, commanding voice, "You take care of this baby." And somehow I managed "I will" from a throat that contained a stone.

He pried Erik from his chest, unwillingly, longingly, as though he was in pain. I held my arms open to receive my baby, and again the gentleman addressed me: "God bless you, M'am. You've given me my Christmas gift." I said nothing more than a muttered, "Thanks."

With Erik in my arms, I ran for the car. Dennis wondered why I was crying and holding Erik so tightly. And why I was saying, "My God, forgive me. Forgive me."

I would like to suggest that the meaning of Christmas is Erik. Erik is God. Erik is Christmas. Erik is God's arms, zeal, and passion for us tattered bums with our tattered lives, our tattered hurts, our tattered relationships, and our tattered sins. Erik is two arms determined to break into our lives.

Erik is a fierce little baby who makes no distinctions but would embrace the least likely. And that's what Christmas is about. It's' an enormously unrelenting kind of a feast. It is not sentimentality. It is not soft. It is as hot and hard as any romance. It is God's fulfilled desire to be with us. And that's why we celebrate.

If God is not with us and if God has not embraced our tattered lives, woe is us. There is no hope. And there is no light, only darkness and despair. And we are here tonight out of fruitless hope, pressured routine, or empty sentimentality.

But if we are here because of love and we are here like ragtag shepherds to kneel and rejoice, then we have caught Christmas's meaning: Emmanuel, the passionate God, has had his way and has hugged us fiercely.

William J. Bausch

Maggie

*T*he rain was lashing down and visibility was so poor as I swung the car round towards the exit of the church car park on a dark December evening, that I nearly didn't see her as she tried to flag me down. "Can yer give us a lift 'ome?" came a voice out of an old and rainswept face which peered into mine through the car window. She had almost finished lowering herself into the passenger seat before I had time to reply. "240, Jackson Street," she said, confidently ignoring the conventional icebreakers normally employed by beggars of lifts.

A moment or two passed before I realised that my self-invited passenger was one of the town's celebrities, better known to St Helens folk than any of its Rugby League stars. Maggie was the sort of soul you find in all the towns and cities of England I'm sure. Recognised by all and shunned by most, they wander from church to church during the day looking for warmth, shelter from the rain, a bit of human company and a bit of Divine consolation.

Everyone knows them and nobody does. I had often wondered who she was and what story lay behind the shuffling, bewhiskered little creature whose presence had often pricked my conscience. But pride had always got the better of both curiosity and a pricked conscience – someone might have seen me talking to her!

Anyway, tonight I had no choice, like it or not, there she was sitting on the blue velour seats of my new car. I kept the window open, preferring a wet shoulder to the combination of natural aromas which my passenger had brought with her. It was a short journey to Jackson Street and I had already planned on going for a pint with the lads. "Are yer comin' in for a cuppa tea, then?" I'd already put the gear stick into first when the invitation came. I just couldn't bring myself to say no, though heaven knows I didn't fancy the idea very much. A cuppa tea never killed anybody. But this time it nearly did!

Maggie's house was a spectacle of disarray, and the aroma she had left in the car came in a more concentrated form inside no 240. I stood by her in the kitchen as she boiled the water in an ancient saucepan and later poured it into a well stained bone china tea cup. I've never drunk a cup of tea so slowly or so unwillingly, but drink it I did. The wallpaper in Maggie's house was partly retained by the original paste, and partly by drawing pins which held cheap and distasteful pictures of various saints. On seeing me glance at her religious art gallery, Maggie began to indicate her special favourites. "That's St Joseph and this is St Martin. Here's the Sacred Heart, and this," she pointed with pride to a small picture which hung at least 30 degrees out of true, "this is Our Lady of Lourdes – a marvellous woman!" At this I started to laugh, at the same time trying to think of a good explanation for my outburst. None was required. A second cup of tea was offered and refused. It was only then that it struck me how cold it was. In the grate were old ashes and some singed newspapers. "Shall I make a fire for you, Maggie?" "Yis, but I've not much coal." As I left that evening, the fire was burning up nicely and the desire for a pint with the lads had long passed.

That wasn't the last time I saw Maggie. A week or so later I found myself knocking at no. 240 again. Maggie was obviously distressed and told me that the house had been broken into. "Do you know who did it, Maggie?" I asked. "Yis, it wuz 'im," she replied immediately. "Who?" I asked, impressed that the culprit had been found so quickly. "The gentleman next door but one," she replied without batting an eyelid. The vision of this 'gentleman', a Raffles type figure, tail-coated and white-gloved breaking into Maggie's coal shed was too much for me. My uncontrolled laughter distressed Maggie who thought I was laughing at her misfortune. Changing the subject was the only escape route. "Why don't you ask for a home help Maggie?" The suggestion was dismissed out of hand and without explanation.

It was Christmas Eve before I saw Maggie again. It must have been about 9.30 in the evening when she came to the door. For the first time I noticed some self-pity in her as I sat down cautiously in the veteran three-legged armchair. She had been weeping and the house seemed in greater turmoil than ever. The fire was dead again and as I got up and made to fill the coal bucket, she stopped me. "There is none," she said, sobbing. It was cold, in fact there was a light dusting of snow outside and there wasn't even a stick of wood in the coal shed. But where do you find coal at 10.30 p.m. on Christmas Eve? Already the Christmas Eve drink had gone by the board, but it seemed insignificant in the extreme at that moment. If Christmas had any meaning at all, then it was to be found in Maggie's cold and chaotic house, not in the lounge of the Red Cat.

Maggie wasn't 'getting on' with the neighbours too well, she never did, so it was pointless asking them. Everyone else I knew had long since abandoned coal fires in favour of gas or electric heating. Then I remembered a family in Wigan who still had a coal fire. If I'd thought too much beforehand about the inconvenience of calling on someone at 11.00 p.m. on Christmas Eve I might not have gone. But instead I just bundled Maggie into the car (where at least it was warm) and drove the ten miles or so to Wigan.

The family did show more than mild surprise at my request at such an odd time for a bucketful of coal, but they gave it willingly and we returned to no 240 pleased at our success. Maggie wasn't given to thanking people profusely, or come to that, to thanking them at all. But the thanks came from the smile that invaded her face as we watched he fire burn up in the hearth. A gang of boisterous youths passed by outside to remind us that the world was celebrating Christmas. Inside no 240 Jackson Street the celebrations were of a different kind.
Frank Johnson

The Snowstar

L ike all elves, Alfirion loved to dance.

One day, during the six-month night of the North Pole where she lived, she was dancing with her many friends upon a big, big sheet of black ice. It sparkled in the starlight.

Everlind, one of the elf-men, suddenly called out: "What's that?"

Alfirion was the first to come and see it. Cupped in between two rocks as black as coal was a shining snowflake. It was exquisite. It was perfect. Each of its fern-like arms was exactly the same and formed of the same intricate, woven, curious pattern. As soon as she saw it, Alfirion loved it. She knelt quietly and watched it.

The other elves came laughing up to her. They glided and skipped upon the ice. They too looked at the snowflake.

"Lovely, isn't it?" they said one to another.

And then, laughingly, they went back to their dance. Alfirion went with them. But every now and then, she would leave the dance and return to her snowflake – she already thought of it as hers.

It was like no snowflake she had ever seen before. It gleamed with its own light, there among the shadows. It was like a six-pointed star: brighter than a diamond, clearer than a tear.

When all the elves went back into the mountain, Alfirion followed behind, a little at a distance. She had scooped up the snowflake and placed it inside a box of ice which she kept cold by magic. She hid the box in a little pocket inside her belt.

Now it was time to work again. Christmas was coming soon and there was much to do. They had thousands of toys and wonderful things to make for Father Christmas to take as presents to all the boys and girls in the world. The elves liked making things almost as much as dancing, so they would often sing as they worked. And today Alfirion sang loudest, thinking of the snowstar as she called the beautiful snowflake hidden in her belt.

They were in the middle of a song when a great silence suddenly dropped upon the hall in which they worked. Father Christmas had entered, and he looked worried.

"What is it? What is it?" cried all he elves together.

Father Christmas stamped some now off his boots and said: "I'm thinking about a little boy who is very ill."

The elves went very quiet. Normally, they would joke and accuse Father Christmas of smelling of reindeer and laughing too loud and ask him why he bothered wearing those silly red clothes. But Father Christmas was not laughing now. A tiny tear perched in the corner of each eye, like a pearl in an oyster.

"He's quite small," he went on, "only four years old. And he's a poor mother's only child. All he needs to get well again is something beautiful for Christmas."

"We'll make something!" cried Haldred, one of the elf-men, and an elf-maiden named Felladel called out, "Or we'll find it!"

Alfirion went red. She put her hand to her belt and thought, 'I love my snowstar; I'm not giving it to anyone for anything. I love it too much.' She looked shyly sideways to see whether anyone had noticed that she was blushing. But none of the elves was watching her.

On what they called the next day, which only meant that it was the time after they had slept for a while, all the elves hurried back to work. They were very excited. Each one thought of how he or she would make something especially beautiful for the sick little boy.

But amidst the singing of the busy elves, Alfirion was silent. She did not really know why she felt as she did. But something was nagging at her. The only moments of calm she had were when, during the breaks, she would scamper off into a corner and wait for the other elves to leave the hall. Then, alone with the work-benches and hammers and saws and glue and needles and thread and the loud echo there was when the hall was empty, Alfirion would open her magic box of ice. There, beautiful as ever, glittered her snowstar. She would sigh, close the box, and go quietly outside to join the merry-making of the other elves.

Despite peeping into the box, though, she was quite gloomy by the end of the day, which was something so strange for an elf that the others noticed it.

She was just explaining to Everlind, for the fourth time, that nothing was the matter, when Father Christmas himself came in. He too looked gloomy. "Well," he said, "have you found anything yet? The little boy was worse today. His mother can only stop weeping without stopping by working without stopping."

Haldred and Felladel called out together, "Come over here and see what we've made!"

Father Christmas went to them. They had made a huge purple tortoise. It could talk. He shook his head

"It's wonderful," he said, "but the little boy won't like that."

Then all the elves brought all the things they had made: train sets and farms and balls and dinosaurs and spaceships and fluffy toys; yet to each of them Father Christmas said the same: "It's wonderful, but the little boy won't like that."

Alfirion, like all the others, was disheartened. They went back to work singing a subdued song. Father Christmas stood near the hall's huge wooden doors, his head down. Then he looked up suddenly and said in a decided voice: "It must be something that somebody cares for more than anything else. Only that will cure the little boy."

Alfirion felt as if a blow had struck her. Now she realised what it was that had been nagging and nagging and making her unhappy. It was that she ought to give her snowstar as a Christmas present to her little boy, but she hated the thought. She certainly was not going to give up her treasure. Why should she? It was hers.

The next day was hectic. It was Christmas Eve and everything had to be finished. The elves, however, still found time to try making things for the little boy. And Alfirion would gloomily creep off to peep at her snowstar. It was always ready to shine out in her little box, beautiful and burning like a little white sun.

When it was time for Father Christmas to load his sleigh, all the elves ran to help him. They showed Father Christmas the things they had made for the little boy: whole cities and marvellous birds and trees formed out of jewels.

Father Christmas said the same:

"It's wonderful, but the little boy won't like that."

And then he added with a sigh: "It has to be something that somebody cares for more than anything else."

Alfirion scraped the snow with her toe. She felt bitterly sad. 'But,' she said to herself 'I'm not going to give up my snowstar.'

All the elves said 'good-bye' to Father Christmas, and singing a Christmas song, trooped back into the mountain. The reindeer jingled their harness as the sleigh began to move.

Alfirion still stood on the same spot. There was a little trough in the snow in front of her feet, worn away by her toe.

The first reindeer was about to mount up into the sky when she called: "Father Christmas!"

He stopped suddenly and turned. "Why, Alfirion!" he exclaimed in amazement. "What is it?"

"Perhaps the little boy would like this. It's my snowstar. I keep it cold in a magic box of ice. It's the most beautiful thing I've ever seen.

And, indeed, as she hand it to him, the snowstar did seem to be blazing far more brilliantly than ever before.

"It's wonderful," said Father Christmas, "and I'm sure the little boy will like it. Thank you, thank you."

And he laughed a great laugh, such that it seemed as if all the stars shook in the sky with gladness. Then his reindeer leapt up into the sky, and he was gone. Alfirion was left completely alone.

"I wonder what I did that for?" she said to herself.

Just then a gust of wind blew a spray of snow from a boulder nearby. The snow spun and swirled in the starlight.

"Oh, look!" she gasped. "I never noticed before how all the millions and millions of snowflakes are so beautiful. First I had only one, but now see! I have millions of them!" And she kicked up a shower of snow from the ground. Then, with a dance that made the snowflakes twirl around in the air about her, she returned laughing into the mountain.

Callan Slipper

Zossimar's Christmas Eve

*I*t was always cold up in the mountains at that time of year. 'December is a hard month,' thought Zossimar as he trudged through the snow. The cold seemed to tear at him, despite his many layers of clothing. It was worse every year, but now that he was old he felt it more than ever.

He was tired too. It would be good to get back home, even though there was nobody there to meet him any more. His wife had died earlier that year, finally worn out by the hard life they had lived. They had never had any children.

'Spoils Christmas that does, not having any children around,' he said to himself. 'No one to run about all excited over their presents.' He smiled to himself as he remembered Christmas when he was a child, so long ago. 'Don't suppose I'll have much of a Christmas this year either.' And in his heart of hearts he thought that God, in whom he believed fervently, had forgotten about him.

His thoughts were so gloomy that he did not even notice the moonlight sparkling through the snow-laden pine trees. It would have taken his breath away. But he did notice something else, scuffling sound just off the path to his right. Instantly alert, he pulled his rifle off his shoulder and pointed it at the bushes. His eyes took in everything of the chilly night, even the white icicles on the twigs. Silence. He waited. The scuffling came again, this time combined with a sound like a sob. His heart beat wildly. He decided to take a closer look. Cautiously, he stepped forward. Without a sound, he moved around the bushes. All was still.

Zossimar was not sure what he feared, but he feared something. He had had enough experiences out alone on the mountain to know that you could never be quite safe.

92

As he peered into a small clearing full of bright moonlight and deep shadows, he held his rifle ready to fire. This was where the noises seemed to lead. A dark bundle moved beneath a tree trunk. A sound like weeping. Zossimar pointed his rifle. And then he saw what it was: an exhausted young woman dressed in rags, clutching a baby.

"Oh!" he exclaimed. And the young woman turned a frightened glance at him. She said nothing. Her lips were blue with the cold, and red marks round her eyes showed where she had been crying.

"In trouble are you?" Zossimar asked. But the woman just stared at him.

"Lost your tongue?" said Zossimar. The woman shrank back, almost imperceptibly, from the hint of harshness in his voice. She still said nothing. Zossimar heaved a sigh. He did not know what to do, but he was certain that the woman and her child could not survive the night in the cold.

"You'd better get to somewhere warm. Don't you know it's Christmas tomorrow? Your people will be looking for you to celebrate the holiday. Why don't you go home, little mother?"

The woman just stared at him and however he tried to talk to her, the answer was always the same. She did not appear to understand the words he said. In the end, he made a decision:

"You'd better come home with me. It's not much, but at least I have a fire and you'll be out of the wind."

Although she gave no sign of understanding what Zossimar had said, the woman did not object to his helping her up and leading her, clutching her baby, to the path. She stumbled a little, so Zossimar took her by the arm and helped her through the trees. The sound of their footsteps crunched on the snow, and as they walked together the moon made a pool of silver light around the three of them.

"We've not far to go now," said Zossimar. The woman began shivering.

"My, my! You've got a fever!" he said. And as soon as they reached he one-roomed cottage where he lived, he took her and laid her down in a corner of his own bed, the only one in the place, and began warming some milk for her and her baby. He looked outside at the moon and thought that it would soon be time to go to midnight mass to welcome the new-born Christ-child. 'But I'd better look after this mother and child first', he added to himself.

When he returned to the woman, she was shaking violently, and great beads of sweat clustered across her brow. The baby began to wail.

"You're very ill, little mother," said Zossimar, and very gently he took the baby from her. She did not notice. He walked up and down with the weeping infant in his arms. After a minute, it occurred to him that the child was probably hungry, so he took the bottle and teat that usually served for goat kids, and fed it. Soothed, the child grew quiet. Then he laid it in a rag-filled box near the fire and went to the bed. Putting one hand behind the mother's head, and holding a cup with the other, he fed her.

"You're very, very ill little mother. Rest here a while and I'll get a doctor," he said after a time. "Just you wait though, no wandering. I'll not be long."

He built the fire up and put the table in front of it, to make sure that if she got up she would not fall into the flames, put the child near its mother, and with a feeling of sad compassion stirring inside him, went into the cold night air.

Going down the mountainside, he could hear the distant church bells ringing. He considered going immediately to church. 'No time for that,' he thought and added wryly, 'not even that amount of Christmas for me. If I don't get a doctor soon, who knows what'll happen to that woman?' And he hurried on.

The doctor, who had known Zossimar for many years and liked him, came quickly. When they got there, nothing had moved in the room since Zossimar had left it, except that the woman, obviously feeling too hot in her fever, had tossed off the blankets with which Zossimar had covered her. She now lay shivering and staring at the door. The doctor examined her.

"She'll live, just about," he said to Zossimar. "But she'll need looking after. It's just as well you found them both: they would never have survived the night. Now look," he said as he drew a bottle of medicine from his bag, "give her this every four hours until her fever goes down. After that a small dose three times daily will be sufficient. On no account miss giving it to her, that could be fatal."

Then, as promptly as he had come, the doctor left. He wanted to go home to his family and join in the festivities. They would miss him if he was not there. Zossimar, alone with the woman and child, settled down in his chair to begin a night's vigil watching over them. He dozed off. He was awakened in the first light of dawn by the cooing and gurgling sound of a contented baby. He looked up.

There, sitting up in his bed, was the young woman, with the baby cradled in her arms. She seemed completely better. She smiled at Zossimar, with a smile that made him melt within, and suddenly something dawned on him. Here was his Christmas. Here was his present. His gift was in giving, in caring for this child and its mother. God had not forgotten him, but had come bearing gifts. Zossimar smiled, lighter at heart than he had been for many months.

Callan Slipper

Skylarks and Horses

*T*he nurse tidying the bed in the white hospital room tried to smile. But the man lying in the bed frowned at her and said nothing. And this was a good day: it was Christmas. Other days he could normally manage to make some hurtful comment as soon as you came through the door.

As he watched the nurse busy around him, Harkon Brice thought how people always found the most inconvenient moment to do anything. Not that he was at all sure when it would be convenient to have his bed made. But he was certain that the time was not now. However, he said to himself, such are the joys of the 'hozzie' which made him think of why he was there in the first place: he had fallen off a 'hossie'. Awful pun! he thought, but it brought to mind someone else who used to like joking, someone a long time ago.

The campfire was bright, though several logs let off thick grey puffs of smoke. It had been a wet summer and everything was damp. They were sitting in silence, with their caravans huddled on the edges of the light. Occasionally, someone would go inside or come out, but on the whole there was stillness. One of the few other movements came from Harkon's mother, who never stopped working, as she sewed noiselessly by the light of the fire. She was mending a woollen jumper that belonged to Harkon. It had the picture of a horse on it, a picture suitable for horse-mad Harkon.

"It's gettin' late," his mother said in her Norwegian accent. Harkon knew what that meant. He did not move. Ever since his father had left them, his mother had been very strict. Bedtime!

A cheery shape shifted in the shadows. It bristled a white

face with bushy black hair, curling eyebrows, and a beard spreading like raven's wings, into the firelight. Burley. A big man, just like his name.

"Mrs Brice," he said, his voice deep and full of hints of humour, "I wonder could the little man come to my place a moment. I have something to show him."

With his mother's permission Harkon found himself following the big man lumbering slowly through the caravans. Out of the firelight and in the chilly glimmer of the moon, they looked rather sad. Not as bad as they did during the day, when the ravages of the weather had stripped paint and rotted the woodwork and pushed together clutters of litter beneath the wheels, so that the whole place looked like it truly was, a dump yard, a place where the Council with nowhere else to put the homeless would house them and then quietly forget about the problem.

"In we go little man," said Burley as he placed a gnarled hand, like a crippled claw on the handle. He seemed to have difficulty opening it. Harkon watched, tempted to offer some help. But he was too shy.

The door opened on a warm yellow glow of light. In the midst of the light various shapes began to form themselves as Harkon's eyes adjusted from the darkness: a sink full of washing up, a nightblack window pane behind it, a threadbare carpet, a shelf full of carved wooden objects, mostly birds in flight (seagulls and eagles and soaring skylarks), and at the far end of the room an old woman sitting in a rocking chair quite out of keeping with the cramped space of the caravan, Burley's mother. She was obviously very old and very ill. A grey face and white hair swathed in grey blankets.

"You know Harkon, don't you, mother?"

"Yes, dear."

"He's the one who wants to be a jockey when he grows up."

"I remember."

"Good, well, Harkon, say hello to my mother."

Harkon stuttered a greeting. Mrs Burley smiled at him.

"It's very nice to see you. Pity we don't keep horses here, though!" she said with a wry look. Harkon smiled. She had made him feel at ease.

"No room with this chair of mine, see? Well, make yourself at home." And with that the old woman nodded off to sleep.

"She hasn't got long to live," whispered Burley. He paused to look at her and then turned towards the shelf full of carvings.

"I made them myself. I thought you might like to see them. Beats going to bed, anyway."

Harkon chuckled. Then he stared at the carvings. His gaze was drawn immediately to a tiny wooden skylark, which strained upwards so hard as it flew and sung that it seemed it would burst from its body.

"That's my favourite too," said Burley.

They studied the carvings, talking and joking in whispers for at least twenty minutes, and then Burley announced it was time to go. He was going to have to start getting his mother ready for bed.

"But," said Harkon as he was going out of the door, "all these models are quite old. Haven't you done any new ones?"

"Can't," said Burley. "Too painful."

Harkon looked quizzically at him. So Burley showed him his hands and said with a smile:

"Arthritis."

"Don't you mind?"

"Things come and things go, and so must you! You can come again tomorrow."

Lying in his hospital bed, Harkon remembered those distant days when he had been so young. Now, it seemed, his hopes had come to a sorry end. Certainly he had become a jockey, but after his fall, so near to winning the biggest race of his career, he would never ride in a race again. His right hand had lost three fingers.

He pictured the caravan camp, in all its rundown glory. He recalled visiting Burley fairly often, and making friends with Burley's mother in the few moments when she was able to speak. In particular he remembered once when he met Burley in the early morning. For some reason the incident had always stuck in his mind as significant.

There was mist around. He had been sent by his own mother to the pump to get some water. Burley was already there. Harkon came up, unheard, from behind. Burley's huge frame seemed to be draped over the pump. No water was spouting from it.

"Are you all right?" Harkon had asked. And Burley said nothing. After he had repeated the question Burley stirred.

"Oh, sorry little man. I didn't mean to alarm you. It was just a twinge of discomfort. Me ole limbs aren't what they used to be."

"Aren't you worried?"

"Worried? No. I do what I can. In the end, nothing matters very much, you know."

"Oh," said Harkon trying to look very grown up. Burley grinned.

"Did you hear the one about the abbot, the orange and the kangaroo?"

Harkon could not remember the joke any more, but he did remember that he had laughed until his sides hurt. Well, he was not laughing now. He tried to roll over in his bed, but his broken ribs sent shooting pains all through him. What a way to spend Christmas! At the thought of Christmas, other memories came flooding back of Christmases when he was small. And one memory in particular.

He was sitting in the caravan where he lived with his mother. He had been banned from going out because of something he had done wrong, he could not recall what. It was

Christmas Eve, a couple of weeks before old Mrs Burley died. Everyone knew she was very ill. His mother, who was still cross with him, was banging about in the kitchen part of the caravan as she prepared food for the following day.

"You will never be makin' a horse-rider unless you learn a, er, responsibler attitude."

"Yes, mother."

"Well then, you'd better get doin' some tidyin'." Harkon began, not very successfully: there was so much to do. And as he worked at it he grew more and more angry, because he so loathed cleaning anything up. It was a great relief to him when there came a knock at the door. His mother opened it. There in the grey winter's light stood Burley. He had a package under his arm.

"Come in, Mr Burley," his mother said. "How's your mother?"

"Cheerful, thank you, Mrs Brice," said Burley as he struggled uncomfortably into the caravan. Harkon's mother looked with pity on him. Droplets of sweat had formed on his brow with the effort of walking. The arthritis was taking its toll.

"Christmas is a happy time of year," he said. "So I thought I'd bring something for little Harkon here."

"That's very kind of you, Mr Burley," Harkon's mother said. Harkon himself approached timidly from the back of the caravan.

"Here you are," said Burley handing him the package rather untidily wrapped in brown paper. "There's been a lot of weather recently, eh, Mrs Brice?"

As Burley made his mother laugh with his jokes, Harkon undid the package. The paper fell on the floor as he took out the object inside. His face had a look of something like awe on it. Exquisitely carved was a wooden model of a horse, running free, mane flowing in the wind, neck muscles straining forward, as if nothing could ever hold back the horse's strength. Harkon held his breath.

"Merry Christmas, little man," said Burley, softly.

"You made this yourself?" asked Harkon. Burley nodded. And Harkon said:

"But your hands!"

Burley looked at them and shrugged.

"No matter," he said. "Well, I suppose this matters. I wanted to do it for you."

Harkon could not remember what happened after that. He knew his mother had said what a nice man Burley was, but most people said that anyway. As he lay in the hospital, though, the memory of Burley came lumbering right into the middle of his thoughts. He felt a glow of warmth inside. Turning his head a little he could see the snow begin to fall outside. It made him feel even warmer not to be out in it.

One of the interminable nurses came bustling in: to check his blood pressure or something like that. How he hated to be disturbed, specially as he was enjoying his own thoughts! He was just about to say something really rude when he stopped. He did not want to destroy the warm feeling spread all over his limbs. Instead, he said:

"Merry Christmas!"

The nurse was clearly shocked.

"Oh, merry Christmas!" she said. She smiled. Harkon felt a smile spreading irresistibly across his own face.

Callan Slipper

Albia

*T*he howls outside were strangely familiar, like the screams of his childhood nightmares. The howl of the snow-white wind mixed with another sound, sadder, lonelier, unimaginably hungry, the cry of the monster of the ice wastes of Albia.

He pulled the skin blankets close to him in the half-dark of the cave. At least in the rank-smelling midst of the Albian cave-dwellers, he was safe. Or so it seemed for the moment. Wang 24 Ruphus, of Chinese extraction and from the planet Earth, thought sadly to himself of his plight alone on a distant world and among creatures who were the enemies of all earthlings. He could not understand for what cruel purpose they had captured him. All those who came to this planet had heard the tales of how, ever since hostilities had broken out, the Albians had tortured their prisoners.

Despite that, in capturing him, they had also saved him. He had been cut off from the other miners and their armed guard and was wandering lost in the empty snowlands, when he had suddenly sensed something behind him. He swung round to face it. It was worse than any dream. The monster of the ice wastes was huge, almost shapeless, with an enormous shadowy mouth, but it cast no shadow: the sky shone right through it. He ran and it howled. He ran and ran. How the Albians had found him and hidden him away, he did not know. His memory was only of fear and whiteness and the sound of the pursuing monster.

Wang watched the Albians moving about the cave, cooking and cleaning and making tools. They looked almost human in the twilight, although they were much smaller than people from Earth, and the fine, dense covering of white hair gave their skin a silvery sheen. Wang could see why people argued whether or not they actually were human, perhaps even centuries ago from Earth itself, however unlikely that was.

A little Albian girl came across the cave to him. She had the big blue eyes of all her kind, but it was impossible to say what she was thinking. That of course was one point in the famous argument as to whether the Albians, who were obviously quite clever, were human: did they think? Some philosopher-theologians said if they did, and if they could make free choices and could, therefore, love, then they were made in the image of God, and because of that they were in some way essentially human. Wang had always liked to argue, even though he thought it was really a waste of time.

She offered Wang a warm drink. She was often doing him little acts of kindness. He wondered what the reason was.

"Thank you," he said.

She made a fairly musical but completely incomprehensible noise, which he took to be some sort of language, and away she went again.

Wang seemed to have done something to his leg when he was escaping from the monster. It hurt. He had also mysteriously acquired a mass of bruises all over his body. They hurt whenever he moved, so most of the time he kept still. Every now and then a group of muttering Albians would come to him, make him lie back so he could not see anything, and remove the bandage from his leg. That hurt as well. But Wang could do nothing about it because, apart from being half patient, he knew he was half prisoner as well.

Shortly after Wang had been given the drink, there seemed to be a change in the atmosphere. The cave-dwellers whispered to one another. Every now and then they would look at Wang and glance hurriedly away. Wang's heart began to beat a little faster. He noticed that the Albians were moving more quickly, as if some order had been given.

A small group of snow-covered travellers came in from the outside. They all squeaked and murmured to one another. Then the whole group sat down to eat. The little girl who had given Wang the hot drink came over and handed him some food. He had had it before. It tasted revolting. It was like glue with a rotten flavour, probably made from one of the many large species of insect-like creatures that roamed the dark recesses of the planet. But anything was better than starvation, and so he said, "Thank you," again and wondered whether they were actually trying to poison him.

The little girl stood by him as he ate. He was not sure but he thought she might have been smiling. When he finished she patted his brow and went a few paces away and began to eat her own meal of the same dreadful substance.

Before he knew what was happening, another secret order seemed to have been passed among the little cave-dwellers. Four of them grabbed him, tugging him to his feet. He tried to resist, but others joined the first four. The little girl stood in front of him. She bared her teeth and made noises. Wang felt even more scared. The little girl took Wang by the hand, while the others held him by the arms. She stroked his hand. It was clear that she was trying to calm him, but Wang could not tell why. Then she pulled at his hand and it was clear he had to move. The others pushed him. Aching in every muscle, Wang began to talk.

He had heard of things like this. The death march it was called. Sweat broke out on Wang's forehead. He noticed the little girl's big blue eyes staring at him. In the corner of each of them there seemed to be laughter. Wang thought she was mocking him.

All the others in the cave collected up their things and put on extra clothing. As they did so, the little girl left Wang a moment and returned with his heavy outdoor gear. She handed it to him. Rather stiffly, both because of his bruises and because of his fear, he put it on. When he was ready, the Albians pushed him through the leathery flap that covered the cave's entrance out into the white world outside. They all followed.

He did not recognise where he was. The sound outside had the curious mix of muffledness and clarity, which he had become used to in the snow-laden landscape. The Albians pushed him along. Wang's fear grew a little less when he noticed that they were moving at the pace he set. Somehow the care that implied made him feel better. But he was not allowed to stand still or to go back. The little girl stayed close to him. That made him feel just a little less alone and friendless. But, at the same time as fearing for his life, he felt utterly lonely, cut off, almost cast out, from humanity.

They went round a craggy boulder, with some surprisingly vivid green thing growing in its cracks. On the other side they found more Albians waiting for them. They were very different from the first group, much more noisy, and as the two groups joined together, they all began making loud noises. For a while Wang even thought they might be laughing and joking.

Other groups joined them as they went, each group quite different from the last, until they became a huge and colourful band. Wang seemed to be forgotten in the midst of what he was almost certain was a mood of merriment. Had he not been so worried, and so well aware of the danger he was in, he might have thought he was in the middle of a party. Only the little girl and a few Albians who seemed to have been detailed to guard him stayed near.

Then suddenly Wang recognised where they were. A gentle shower of snow was falling as in the distance he saw the earth settlement, the place they called the City of Lights, because lamps of all colours hung from the buildings, twinkling through the clear plastic dome which arched over everything. Then Wang saw a group of soldiers coming out of the City. Perhaps they were coming to rescue him? Was he a hostage? But no, he realised, the soldiers did not even know that the Albians were there or they would never have risked coming out against such a huge number of the enemy.

The Albians had seen the soldiers too. They were silent. They carried on walking, but with a sense of tension in the air. They did not seem to be going directly to the City at all, but were ignoring it and the soldiers. Wang thought this odd, because they were supposed to be savage and fond of fighting.

He was wondering about this when he saw the soldiers stop quite still. They had seen a very small, unarmed group of Albians that was coming towards the large party Wang was with. To his amazement, the soldiers charged at the unarmed Albians and began shooting. The large party let out a howl of dismay. The soldiers suddenly saw they were there. They stopped firing and stared at the huge number of Albians, more than anyone had ever seen together in one place. The soldiers were rigid with fear. Wang was speechless. He was angry because of the brutality he had witnessed and worried because he was certain that the soldiers could now be attacked and made to pay for their cruelty. The little girl at his side stared dumbly at him as if deeply shocked herself by what his people had done.

Then, slowly, the very small group of Albians began to walk again, carrying the injured or those who had fallen. The larger group waited, in a quiet so quiet it seemed almost solid. What was going to happen? The soldiers stood unmoving, the City of lights behind them, their guns at the ready.

The small group walked in front of the soldiers. They walked within easy range of their guns. They walked until they reached the large group which stood, waited, and still did not attack. The two groups joined together. As one huge group they faced the soldiers. Then, without speaking, they all turned and began to walk again. The little girl tugged at

Wang's hand and he, willingly, began to walk with them. The soldiers in the distance watched, amazed. The Albians outnumbered them and were simply walking away.

Wang's mind was dizzy with thoughts. He could not understand what had happened. The Albians seemed to have shown more humanity and kindness than the humans, not only when attacked but also, when he thought about it, to himself. They had saved him and, as he now gradually realised, had treated him with nothing but care.

He looked up from his thoughts and saw that the Albians were tending to their injured as they moved. And bit by bit, to his surprise, the mood of merriment began to return.

Together the huge group crossed the ice and came to a soaring outcrop of rock. There was a massive cave mouth before them, within view of the City of Lights but which, oddly enough, no one in the earth settlement seemed to know about. They went inside.

In the darkness Wang could sense the presence of many other Albians. He could not see anything. The little girl took his hand. They wound their way down a long path and came into a cavern lit by a soft glow and larger than the biggest cathedral on earth. The hushed murmur of thousands of Albians washed its sides. In the centre was a space with something in it. At the same moment the Albians all began to make a sound, which to Wang's ears seemed quite musical. What a strange people they are, he thought, no longer afraid.

Then his eyes focussed on what was in the middle of the cavern: laid on a pile of golden straw was the tiny shape of a baby, earthling or Albian he was not sure. Gathered round it were the forms of the various creatures that dwelt on Albia and even, to Wang's shock, the shape of the monster of the ice wastes. As the Albians sang, they and the forms all seemed to move together. Wang's eyes played tricks on him and it seemed to him that everything bowed, bowed down low, bowed to the shape of the baby.

It was then with a pang of realisation that Wang under-stood what was happening. According to Earth's calendar today had to be somewhere close to 25th December. The Albians were celebrating Christmas. Christmas! How the thought of it made him yearn for home! He turned and looked at the little girl who had helped him and led him through the wastes and darkness. There was no doubt in his mind now that she was smiling. She looked at him with the light of Christmas in her eyes. It seemed to Wang that he could see the entire universe there: animals, planets and plants, and with them the whole of humankind.

Callan Slipper

Part Six

St Stephen
and
the Holy Innocents

St Stephen and King Herod

Saint Stephen was a clerk
   King Herod's hall,
And served him with bread and cloth
   As every king befall.

Stephen out of kitchen came
   With boar's head on hand
He saw a star was fair and bright
   Over Bethlehem stand.

He cast adown the boar's head
   And went into the hall;
'I forsake thee, Herod.
   And thy works all.'

'I forsake thee King Herod,
   And thy works all,
There is a child in Bethlehem born
   Is better than we all.'

'What aileth thee, Stephen?
   What is thee befall?
Lacketh thee either meat or drink
   In King Herod's hall?'

'Lacketh me neither meat nor drink
   In King Herod's hall;
There is a child in Bethlehem born
   Is better than we all.'

'What aileth thee Stephen?
    mad or hast grown wroth?
Lacked thee either gold or fee
    Or any rich cloth?'

'Lacketh me neither gold nor fee
    Nor cloth nor things of greed.
There is a child in Bethlehem born
    Shall help us in our need.'

'That is all so true Stephen,
    All so true I know,
As if the capon in this dish
    Should come to life and crow.'

That word was not so soon said,
    That word in that hall,
The capon crew Christus natus est
    Among the lords all.

'Rise up, my true tormentors,
    By two and all by one,
Lead Stephen here out of this town
    And stone him with stone.'

They took Stephen
    And stoned him on the way,
And therefore is his even
    On Christ's own day.

An early English ballad

St Stephen's Day

Spoken by Naaman of the Gadarenas.

I had a friend from the North Country, and his name was Stephen; and because he proclaimed Jesus as the Son of God, he was led to the market place and stoned.

And when Stephen fell to earth he outstretched his arms as if he would die as his Master had died. His arms were spread like wings ready for flight. And when the last gleam of light was fading in his eyes, with my own eyes I saw a smile upon his lips. It was a smile like breath that comes before the end of winter for a pledge – a promise of Spring.

Khalil Gibran
(1883 – 1931)

Our Lord and Our Lady

They warned Our Lady for the Child
That was Our Blessed Lord,
And She took Him into the desert wild,
Over the camel's ford.

And a long song She sang to Him
And a short story told:
And She wrapped Him in a woollen cloak
To keep Him from the cold.

But when Our Lord was grown a man
The Rich they dragged Him down,
And they crucified Him in Golgotha,
Out and beyond the Town.

They crucified Him on Calvary,
Upon an April day;
And because He had been Her little Son
She followed Him all the way.

Our Lady stood beside the Cross,
A little space apart,
And when She heard Our Lord cry out
A sword went through Her Heart.

They laid Our Lord in a marble tomb,
Dead in a winding sheet.
But Our Lady stands above the world
With the white Moon at Her feet.

Hilaire Belloc
(1870 – 1953)

They Confess Christ

*T*he great king is born as a tiny infant. Wise men are led to him from afar. They come to adore one who still lies in a manger but reigns over heaven and earth. When the wise men announce the birth of a king, Herod is troubled and wants to kill him, lest he should lose his own throne. And yet if he believed in him he would reign here securely, and in the Life beyond would reign without end.

Herod, why are you afraid when you hear that the king has arrived. He does not come to usurp your place; he comes to conquer the devil. You do not understand this and so you are in a frenzy, mad with rage, your determination to destroy the one infant whom you seek makes you inhumanly indifferent to the deaths of so many others.

No pity for sorrowing mothers deters you, no sympathy for fathers weeping as their sons are carried to the grave. Nor are you held back by the sobs and crying of the little victims themselves. You slay those little ones because fear in your heart slays you. You think, 'If only I succeed in my purpose, mine will be long life.' But in reality you are seeking to murder Life itself.

He, the source of grace, small yet immense, lies in a manger, and terrifies you on your throne. Unknown to you, he works through you to complete his plans and to free souls from captivity to the devil. Already he has received the offspring of people at enmity with him into the company of his adopted children.

Though they know it not, these little ones die for Christ and their parents are mourning the death of martyrs. The Christ-child has made babies, who are unable to talk, fitting witnesses to himself. This is how he reigns who had come to reign in no other way. Already the liberator sets free, the Saviour offers salvation.

Herod, in your ignorance of this you rage and tremble. But, unknown to you, even as you rage against this little one you are serving him.

How great was the grace thus bestowed. Not through merits of their own did those infants conquer the great adversary. They could not speak, yet they confessed Christ. Helpless to enter the battle, they still carried off the palm of victory.

St Quodvultdeus
(d. 387)

To the Innocents

O ur King is eagerly ready
to welcome the blood-witness of the Innocents.
Angels gather in chorus singing highest praise,
yet the clouds cry out in pain over the Innocents' blood.
Because of his malice, the Tyrant has suffocated
in the heavy sleep of death.
And the clouds cry out in pain over the Innocents' blood.
Glory be to the Father, the Son, and Holy Spirit.
And the clouds cry out in pain over the Innocents' blood.

Hildegard of Bingen
(1098 – 1179)

Hymn to the Holy Innocents

H ail! Flowers of martyrdom, all hail!
Like rosebuds torn by an untimely gale
your lives you gave.

When cruel Herod would have slain
The infant Christ, you by your pain
defied his plan.

You gave your lives for Christ,
you were his earliest sacrifice, your toys
the martyr's crown.

Told that the King of kings was here
The worried tyrant cried in fear:
"Slave, take up arms;

"Seek out male infants; let no ploy
Of nursing mother spare her boy
from instant death."

The destroyer raging with sword drawn
Assailed the bodies of the newly-born
and tore apart their life.

O ghastly sight! Could there be space
On those tiny limbs for the killer to place
his murderous blow?

What use was this so barbarous deed?
Christ from the shedding of his fellows' blood
himself escaped unharmed.

Prudentius
(348 – 410)

Part Seven

The Epiphany

When Herod Heard

*I*n the time of King Herod, after Jesus was born in Bethlehem of Judea, wise men from the East came to Jerusalem, asking, "Where is the Child who has been born King of the Jews? For we observed his star at its rising, and we have come to pay him homage." When King Herod heard this, he was frightened, and all Jerusalem with him; and calling together all the chief priests and scribes of the people, he inquired of them where the Messiah was to be born. They told him, "In Bethlehem of Judea; so far it has been written by the prophet: 'And you Bethlehem, in the land of Judah, are by no means least among the rulers of Judah; for from you shall come a ruler who is to shepherd my people Israel.' "

Then Herod secretly called for the wise men and learned from them the exact time when the star had appeared. Then he sent them to Bethlehem, saying, "Go and search diligently for the child; and when you have found him, bring me word so that I may also go and pay him homage." When they heard the king, they set out; and there ahead of them, went the star that they had seen at its rising, until it stopped over the place where the child was. When they saw that the star had stopped, they were overwhelmed with joy. On entering the house, they saw the child with Mary his mother; and they knelt down and paid him homage. Then, opening their treasure chests, they offered him gifts of gold, frankincense and myrrh. And having been warned in a dream not to return to Herod, they left for their own country by another road.

Matthew 2: 1-12

Christ the King

*T*he Epiphany is a season especially set apart for adoring the glory of Christ. The word may be taken to mean the manifestation of His glory, and leads us to the contemplation of Him as King upon His throne in the midst of His court, with His servants around Him, and His guards in attendance. At Christmas we commemorate His grace; and in Lent His temptation; and on Good Friday His sufferings and death; and on Easter Day His victory; and on Ascension His return to the Father; and in Advent we anticipate His second coming.

And in all of these seasons He does something, or suffers something; but in the Epiphany and the weeks after it, we celebrate Him, not as on His field of battle, or in His solitary retreat, but as an august and glorious King; we view Him as the Object of our worship. Then only, during His whole earthly history, did He fulfil the type of Solomon, and held (as we may say) a court, and received the homage of His subjects, viz, when He was an infant. His throne was His undefiled Mother's arms; His chamber of state was a cottage or a cave; the worshippers were the wise men of the East, and they brought presents, gold, frankincense, and myrrh.

All around and about Him seemed of earth, except to the eye of faith; one note alone had He of divinity. As great men of this world are often plainly dressed, and look like other men, all but as having some one costly ornament on their breast or on their brow; so the Son of Mary in His lowly dwelling, and in an infant's form, was declared to be the Son of God Most High, the Father of Ages, and the Prince of Peace, by His star; a wonderful appearance which had guided the wise men all the way from the East, even unto Bethlehem.
John Henry Newman (1801 – 1890)

Hymn for Epiphany

M other Mary, still maiden, rejoicing,
      her Son at this trifle brought to birth.
This she spoke to Him, Maker of all things,
      God of Ages new-born on this earth.

"Lofty Monarch, why bother with beggars?
      Creator of Heaven, with earth?
Did you long for a cave and a manger,
      instead of a palace, for birth?
Other infants inherit rich acres,
      you only a place of no worth.
I could find but the loan of a stable,
      God of Ages new-born on this earth.

"Yet there seek you now kings from Chaldaea
      come to worship you, bowing the head,
Persian sages whose star-centred learning
      over desert and mountain have led.
Bid them enter! No shame be the fewness
      of worldly possessions; their dearth
Is our wealth, having you for our treasure,
      God of Ages new-born on this earth."

Jesus answered: "I came with them coming.
      My Word was the star gave them light.
You therefore yourself bid them enter
      and worship as seems to them right."
So Mary his Mother, yet maiden,
      rejoicing still more at His birth,
Brought them into the cave to adore Him,
      God of Ages new-born on this earth.

So they offered Him gifts from their treasures,
      gold, incense and myrrh they had brought.
"Pray accept these," they cried, "as from Abel
      his offering, not Cain's, was once sought."
Mary, joyful, joined in with their voices:
      "More precious than all be their worth!
May they move you to bless all creation,
      God of Ages new-born on this earth."

Romanos the Hymnodist
(490 – 560)

The Three Kings

Three Kings came riding from far away,
    Melchior and Gaspar and Baltasar;
Three Wise Men out of the East were they.
And they travelled by night and they slept by day,
    For their guide was a beautiful, wonderful star.

The star was so beautiful, large, and clear,
    all the other stars of the sky
Became a white mist in the atmosphere,
And by this they knew that the coming was near
    Of the Prince foretold in the prophecy.

Three caskets they bore on their saddle-bows,
    Three caskets of gold with golden keys;
Their robes were of crimson silk with rows
Of bells and pomegranates and furbelows,
    Their turbans like blossoming almond-trees.

And so the Three Kings rode into the West,
    Through the dusk of night, over hill and dell,
And sometimes they nodded with beard on breast
And sometimes talked, as they paused to rest,
    With the people they met at some wayside well.

"Of the child that is born," said Baltasar,
    "Good people, I pray you, tell us the news;
For we in the East have seen his star,
And have ridden fast, and have ridden far,
    To find and worship the King of the Jews."

And the people answered, "You ask in vain;
     We know of no king but Herod the Great!"
They thought the Wise Men were men insane,
As they spurred their horses across the plain,
     Like riders in haste, and who cannot wait.

And when they came to Jerusalem,
     Herod the Great, who had heard this thing,
Sent for the Wise Men and questioned them;
And said, "Go down unto Bethlehem,
     And bring me tidings of this new king."

So they rode away; and the star stood still,
     The only one in the gray of morn;
Yes, it stopped, – it stood still of its own free will,
Right over Bethlehem on the hill,
     The city of David, where Christ was born.

And the Three Kings rode through the gate and the guard,
     Through the silent street, till their horses turned
And neighed as they entered the great inn-yard;
But the windows were closed, and the doors were barred,
     And only a light in the stable burned.

And cradled there in the scented hay,
     In the air made sweet by the breath of kine,
The little child in the manger lay,
The child, that would be king one day
     Of a kingdom not human but divine.

His mother Mary of Nazareth
     Sat watching beside his place of rest,
Watching the even flow of his breath,
For the joy of life and the terror of death
     Were mingled together in her breast.

They laid their offerings at his feet:
     The gold was their tribute to a King,
The frankincense, with its odour sweet,
Was for the Priest, the Paraclete,
     The myrrh for the body's burying.

And the mother wondered and bowed her head,
     And sat as still as a statue of stone;
Her heart was troubled yet comforted,
Remembering what the Angel had said
     Of an endless reign and of David's throne.

Then the Kings rode out of the city gate,
     With a clatter of hoofs in proud array;
But they went not back to Herod the Great,
For they knew his malice and feared his hate,
     And returned to their homes by another way.

Henry Wadsworth Longfellow
(1807 – 1882)

The Gift

*A*s the wise men of old brought gifts
guided by a star
            to the humble birthplace
of the god of love,
            the devils
                        as an old print shows
retreated in confusion.

            What could a baby know
                        of gold ornaments
or frankincense and myrrh,
            of priestly robes
                        and devout genuflections?

But the imagination
            knows all stories
                        before they are told
and knows the truth of this one
            past all defection.

The rich gifts
            so unsuitable for a child
                        though devoutly proffered,
stood for all that love can bring.

            The men were old,
                        how could they know
of a mother's needs
            or a child's
                        appetite?

But as they kneeled
        the child was fed.
                They saw it
and
        gave praise!

A miracle
        had taken place,
                hard gold to love,
a mother's milk!
        Before
                their wondering eyes.

The ass brayed
        the cattle lowed.
                It was their nature.

All men by their nature give praise.
        It is all
                they can do.

The very devils
        by their flight give praise.
                What is death,
beside this?

        Nothing. The wise men
                came with gifts
and bowed down
        to worship
        this perfection.

William Carlos Williams
(1883 – 1963)

Gold, Myrrh and Frankincense

*T*ake Frankincense, O God, take Gold, O King,
Take Myrrh, O Man, from those who can them bring:
Poore I, nor Gold, nor Myrrh, nor Frankincense,
Have to present, such is mine indigence,
Yet will I with these noble Persians bring
Some present still, when I salute my King:

I'll give my selfe. A gift too vile, too base
To be presented to so high a grace.
But thou who all thou tak'st doest better make,
Render me better than thou did'st me take.
My selfe a worme, no man, I give to thee,
Restore my selfe a man, a Saint to me…

Charles Fitz-Geoffrey
(1575 – 1638)

Part Eight

Reflections
on the Mystery

The Wooden Manger

*W*e thought we were honouring Christ when we took away the wooden manger and gave him a silver one instead. But as far as I am concerned, the one taken away is the more valuable one. We'll leave the silver and gold to the pagans; a wooden manger is more becoming to the Christian faith. It's the very one who was born in this stable, who condemns gold and silver. I don't mean to condemn those who have done this to pay him honour, any more than I condemn those who used to cast golden vessels for the Temple. But I do admire the Lord, Creator of the world, who chose to be born for us not surrounded by gold and silver, but a patch of earth.

St Jerome
(342 – 420)

Truth

*T*ruth,
enclosed in the bosom of the father,
was revealed on earth
being enclosed in the womb of a mother.
The Truth
which contains the whole world
came upon earth
and was cradled in a woman's arms?

St Augustine
(354 – 430)

The Eternal Springtime
Will Surely Come

*O*nce only in the year, yet once, does the world which we see show forth its hidden powers, and in a manner manifest itself. Then the leaves come out, and the blossoms on the fruit trees and flowers; and the grass and corn spring up. There is a sudden rush and burst outwardly of that hidden life which God has lodged in the material world. Well, that shows you, as by a sample, what it can do at God's command, when he gives the word. This earth, which now buds forth in leaves and blossoms will one day burst forth into a new world of light and glory, in which we shall see saints and angels dwelling. Who would think, except from his experience of former springs all through his life, who could conceive two or three months before, that it was possible that the face of nature, which then seemed so lifeless, should become so splendid and varied?...

So it is with the coming of that Eternal Spring for which all Christians are waiting. Come it will, though it delay; yet though it tarry, let us wait for it, 'because it will surely come, it will not tarry'. Therefore we say day by day, 'Thy kingdom come', which means, 'O Lord, show thyself; manifest thyself; thou that sittest between the cherubim, show thyself; stir up thy strength and come and help us' (Ps 80). The earth that we see does not satisfy us. What we see is the outward shell of an eternal kingdom; and on that kingdom we fix the eyes of our faith.

Shine forth, O Lord, as when on thy Nativity thy angels visited the shepherds; let thy glory blossom forth as bloom and foliage on the trees. Bright as is the sun, and the sky, and the clouds; green as are the leaves and the fields; sweet as is the singing of the birds; we know that they are not all, and we will not take up with a part for the whole. They proceed from a centre of love and goodness, which is God himself, but they are not his fullness; they speak of heaven, but they are not heaven; they are but as stray beams and dim reflections of his image; they are but the crumbs from the table.

John Henry Newman
(1801 – 1890)

The Ground of the Soul

*W*e have become so used to living a falsehood that we can no longer recognise the truth about ourselves, even when it stares us in the face. Receptivity and openness to God in the Soul's Ground are, in fact, what we were created for; to be like this is to be human in the truest sense; and if we cannot see it so, that is because our normal, everyday lives are lived mainly on a subhuman level. What we call 'normality' is in fact abnormality and sickness. It is a diseased state, which prevents us from being our true selves.

It is precisely this disease that Christ cures through his Incarnation. In becoming Man, he becomes true Man, one in whom the potentialities of the human state are actually realised. Jesus is a creature of flesh and blood like us; he has a human body, heart and emotions, and is therefore subject to all the temptations and weakness which that implies. But, being the supremely normal Man, rather than an abnormal one, these fleshly frailties do not prevent Him from being able to do what human beings are supposed to do – to cast aside these creaturely limitations and plunge into the mystery of God in the Soul's Ground.

In his treatise on Detachment, Eckhart tells us that Christ, in the garden of Gethsemane and on the cross, suffered very intensely in his 'outer man' – that is, as a concrete, fleshly human individual – but remained totally detached and united with God in his 'inner man' which is the Soul's Ground. Since he has done this, it is now possible for us to do it too. In the Incarnation of Christ, God took on 'human nature', entering the Ground of the Man, Jesus. That Ground is common to us all, and Christ is still present within it. If we enter the Ground of the Soul, we shall encounter Christ, God the Son.

Not only shall we encounter the Son; we shall also become the Son ourselves; we shall share in the union which the Son has with the Father, the Spirit and the Divine Ground, the Abyss, the Silent Desert. If we strip away from ourselves all that is accidental, relative and individual in ourselves, we shall attain that 'universal human nature' which has been united to Christ, and the Incarnation will thus become a present reality for us, here and now, in our lives.

> *I say that human nature and man are different. Humanity in itself (i.e. at its deepest and truest, when it is most genuinely itself) is a noble thing; that which is highest in human nature has likeness to the angels and kinship with the Godhead. It is possible for me to obtain the greatest union which Christ had with the Father, provided that I am able to lay aside everything 'which is of this and that' and provided that I can take to myself universal human nature. Therefore all that God ever gave to his only begotten Son he has also given to me as perfectly as to him and not less.*

Now we can see what kind of importance Eckhart thinks Christ had for us. Christ is of central importance because in him is enacted the central mystery of the union between God and Man. This happens through the Incarnation, which has a double aspect. On the one hand, God incarnates in the flesh, as Jesus of Nazareth, born into a particular historical situation. This is what we might call the 'outward' aspect of the Incarnation. Far more important, however, in Eckhart's view, is the 'inward' aspect, whereby God enters universal human nature, the transcendent Ground which is common to all human beings wherever they are in space or time. This aspect is more important because it touches us here and now in the deepest core of ourselves, and transforms our lives.

Concepts of Jesus are also concepts of ourselves. If in Jesus there was an 'inner' and an 'outer' man, so there must be in us. Redemption, salvation, must take both aspects into account, and we, today, in our own spiritual lives, must take them into account. We experience the 'outward' Incarnation by recalling it, through the Church, the sacraments, the Scriptures, the endeavour to live a virtuous life. By these means the outer man is purified, and is freed from his dependence on external stimuli and conditioning. But there has also to be an encounter with the 'inner' Incarnation, by detachment from the external world and by entry into the Ground of the Soul. This is by far the most important aspect, because it is through this alone that real change, transformation and union with God are achieved. The Incarnation then ceases to be merely a historical event in the past which is recalled and applied to our outer lives; it becomes a present event, here and now, which transforms our inner lives. Christ is an irresistible force within us, uniting us with God at this very moment.

Cyprian Smith

Coming

*T*o be crucified
again? To be made friends
with for his jeans and beard?
Gods are not put to death

any more. Their lot now
is with the ignored.
I think he still comes
stealthily as of old,

invisible as a mutation,
an echo of what the light
said, when nobody
attended; an impression

of eyes, quicker than
to be caught looking, but taken
on trust like flowers in the
dark country towards which we go.

R.S. Thomas
(1913 – 2000)

By Love Alone

O God,
who by love alone
art great and glorious,
that art present and livest with us
by love alone:
Grant us likewise
by love to attain another self,
by love to live in others,
and by love to come to our glory,
to see and accompany Thy love
throughout all eternity.

Thomas Traherne
(1636 – 1674)

Acknowledgements

Bausch, William J. : *Christmas Passion*
This chapter is based on an insight of Fr Joseph Nolan in his *Homily Service, The Good News,* and developed by Fr William J. Bausch in his book, *More Telling Stories; Compelling Stories,* copyright 1993, (paper, U.S.$ 9.95) published by Twenty-Third Publications, P.O.Box 180, Mystic Ct 06355. Among the many other books by Fr Bausch is the perennial best-selling *Storytelling: Imagination & Faith.*

Belloc, Hilaire: *Our Lord and Our Lady*
Taken from *Sonnets and Verse* by H. Belloc, Duckworth. Reprinted by permission of The Peters Fraser and Dunlop Group Limited on behalf of The Estate of Hilaire Belloc.
© as printed in the original volume.

Bingen, Hildegard of: *In Praise of Mary* and *To the Innocents*
Translation by Matthew Fox. Used with kind permission of the translator.

Carretto, Carlo: *The God Who Comes*
Taken from: *The God Who Comes* by Carlo Carretto, Orbis Books 1974 & DLT 1974, and used by kind permission of the publishers.

Lewis, C.S.: *Building a Palace, The Way Things Work Now, The Mother of the Lord, The Coming of the Lord, Incarnation Transcends Myth* and *A Jewish Girl*
Taken from *The Business of Heaven* by C.S. Lewis copyright © C.S. Lewis Pte. Ltd 1984. Extracts reprinted by permission.

Lisieux, Therese of: *Christmas Eve*
Taken from *Just for Today* and reprinted with kind permission of Templegate Publishers.

Novak, Miguel: *Christmas Under Martial Law*
Taken from New City, December 1991.

Smith, Cyprian: *The Ground of the Soul*
Taken from *The Way of Paradox* by Cyprian Smith, DLT/Paulist Press, 1987, and reprinted with kind permission of the publishers.

Smith, Stevie: *Saint Foam* **and** *the Holy Child*
Taken from *Me Again* by Stevie Smith and reprinted with kind permission of the publishers: Virago Press, 1981.

Thomas, R.S.: *Coming* **and** *Nativity*
Taken from *Experimenting with an Amen* by R.S. Thomas and used by kind permission of Macmillan Publishers Ltd.

Please Note: We were not able to trace the agents of all contributions in this anthology and apologise for any omissions in the acknowledgements. If new information reaches us, this will be corrected in future editions.